A New Owner's
Guide to
AKITAS

JG-111

Overleaf: Ch. Chiheisen's Take It To The Maxx, top-winning Akita bred by Jim and Debra Stewart and Sylvia Thomas. Owned by the Thomases, J. Machline and M. and C. Schipper.

Title page: Ch. O'BJ Sachette No Okii Yubi, the first American champion in England, bred by the author and sold to England's top breeder, Meg Purnell-Carpenter of Overhill Kennels in Pensford.

Photographers: Alverson Photographers, Inc., Barbara J. Andrews, John Ashbey, Tim Burns, Callea Photography, Middleton Evans, Fox & Cook Photography, Isabelle Francais, Graham Studios, Mrs. Michael Kamer, B. Kurtis Photography, MikRon Dog Photography, Robert Pearcy, Don Petrulis Photography, Ron Reagan, John Seaborn, Robert Smith, Judith E. Strom, Chuck Tatham, James Taylor, Missy Yuhl.

The Publisher acknowledges the contribution of Judy Iby for chapters on the dog sport, health and dental care, identification, traveling and canine behavior.

© 1996 by T.F.H. Publications, Inc.

Distributed in the UNITED STATES to the Pet Trade by T.F.H. Publications, Inc., One T.F.H. Plaza, Neptune City, NJ 07753; distributed in the UNITED STATES to the Bookstore and Library Trade by National Book Network, Inc. 4720 Boston Way, Lanham MD 20706; in CANADA to the Pet Trade by H & L Pet Supplies Inc., 27 Kingston Crescent, Kitchener, Ontario N2B 2T6; Rolf C. Hagen Inc., 3225 Sartelon St. Laurent-Montreal Quebec H4R 1E8; in CANADA to the Book Trade by Vanwell Publishing Ltd., 1 Northrup Crescent, St. Catharines, Ontario L2M 6P5 ; in ENGLAND by T.F.H. Publications, PO Box 15, Waterlooville PO7 6BQ; in AUSTRALIA AND THE SOUTH PACIFIC by T.F.H. (Australia), Pty. Ltd., Box 149, Brookvale 2100 N.S.W., Australia; in NEW ZEALAND by Brooklands Aquarium Ltd. 5 McGiven Drive, New Plymouth, RD1 New Zealand; in Japan by T.F.H. Publications, Japan—Jiro Tsuda, 10-12-3 Ohjidai, Sakura, Chiba 285, Japan; in SOUTH AFRICA by Lopis (Pty) Ltd., P.O. Box 39127, Booysens, 2016, Johannesburg, South Africa. Published by T.F.H. Publications, Inc.
MANUFACTURED IN THE
UNITED STATES OF AMERICA
BY T.F.H. PUBLICATIONS, INC.

A NEW OWNER'S GUIDE TO
AKITAS

BARBARA J. ANDREWS

Contents

The Author and the great
Widow-Maker.

Mad Hatter, the number
one dam of all time.

Akitas love Mini-Bulls. Owner
Debbie Erlemeier.

Akitas and children.

Maurizo Moretto and Target Rose.

ORIGIN of the Akita

No breed book would be complete without myth, and myths would be shapeless unless formed by history. Ironically, each is made more distinct by the shadowy line between fact and fiction. Reviewing the history of the Akita is a necessary step if one is to develop an in-depth relationship with a breed that can be frustratingly "mysterious." Like that of many wolf-spitz breeds, the origin of the Akita presents the first puzzle. Beyond being shrouded in the mists of time, the Akita's beginnings are obscured by a culture that is in itself still a mystery to most Westerners.

In the mountains near her North Carolina home, author Barbara J. Andrews poses with one of the first in a long line of O'BJ Akitas.

For example, we readily accept that an Akita statue signifies good health and prosperity. We even understand that in the Orient such beliefs carry more importance than our almost forgotten superstitions regarding black cats or Mister Crow. The oldest Asian cultures have always placed great value on special canines and the myths that are associated with them. In China, for instance, a pariah dog became a peasant dog, then an artistic concept, and, finally, a representative of a basic belief in what we would call the "supernatural." Today, Foo Dog statues guard the entrance to better-quality restaurants and are found in the lobbies of great financial institutions.

While we are enchanted by such Oriental customs as regards dogs, we are not quite prepared to understand why dogs are still eaten in many Asian countries or why the Japanese were once so fond of "dog sports," which we find

Perhaps the most popular sire of all time, Ch. The Widow-Maker O'BJ was the first owner-handled multiple Best in Show Akita, bred, handled and owned by the author.

absolutely appalling. Turning a hundred dogs loose in an arena as targets for bowmen is hardly entertaining by Western definition.

The practice of dog fighting is as old as the semi-domesticated canine, but some cultures have taken it to great extremes. The sport evolved to new dimensions in Japan during the Kamakura period (1185–1333) under the reign of Shogun Hojo Takatoki. The Satake Clan of Odate City (aka Dog Fighting Capital) crossed the Akita-Matagi-inu with the mastiff-like Tosa in order to increase the abilities of the fighting dog.

The Meiji Period (1867–1912) stretched beyond 1908 when Japan passed ordinances that officially outlawed the fighting of dogs. The Enyukai Club (Garden Party Club), formed in Odate City in 1897, remained in vogue for a number of years after the official ruling. Various clubs hosted fighting tournaments

Japanese type and soundness are alive and well in Ch. O'BJ A-Head of the Game, owned by Howard Carlton.

where eager fans would gather for a full day of entertainment. Although this practice offends dog lovers, and it seems shameful that it was practiced so recently, we should remember that it wasn't until the 1980s that states uniformly forbade the practice of dog fighting and began to prosecute offenders in America.

Westerners don't skin their dogs, but the Japanese have long preserved their favored dogs in that manner. One may also view the stuffed remains of famous Akitas in Japanese museums. On the other hand, we are not so far removed from some aspects of Eastern culture. We can view Trigger, Roy Rogers' famous steed, in more than those delightful Saturday afternoon westerns! Perhaps man has always preserved that which was so close to his heart.

Despite the rather sketchy history of the Akita, we know he served a variety of purposes at different levels of society. As the peasant's dog, he was a hunter. As the sporting partner of royalty, he is said to have hunted with falcons. Although he is reputed to have been a good water retriever, I personally refute that, as I've never known an adult Akita to swim without strong encouragement! Wade or lay down in cool water—of course. Swim for the fun of it or to retrieve anything—no way.

Never bred as sled dogs, Akitas can be trained to pull as demonstrated by Steve and Abbie Schiff's West Camp Akita team.

Dogs with double- or triple-layered weather-resistant coats are usually referred to as Arctic or Nordic type dogs and have always had a history of working for their keep. The oldest authenticated remains of *Canis familiaris*, dated some 11,000 years ago, were found in Iraq and, of all places,

Idaho! Researchers Olsen and Olsen (1977) argue that all domestic dogs descended from the Chinese wolf *(C. l. chanco)* and spread throughout the world as trade routes were established. Many authorities today support that theory. Drawings and other artifacts dating back more than 3,000 years document existence of a wolf-spitz dog throughout Asia. This early domesticated dog evolved into breeds we know as the Chow Chow, Elkhound, husky (generic term) and, of course, the Akita. The Akita's more remote ancestors became identifiable by about 500 BC, and we can trace the Akita-inu as a distinct type through over 300 years of written records.

In the overall process of evolutionary development, the Akita is a new kid on the block but one that has captured the imagination and hearts of thousands of people from both Eastern and Western cultures. Like the dominant force it is, the Akita has become a primary breed within the AKC Working Group classification.

Don't be confused by the Japanese terms "ken" and "inu."
These words are used as suffixes, attached to Japanese breeds
by a hyphen as in Akita-ken or Shiba-inu. Both mean simply
"dog." The Akita, like most other Japanese breeds, derives his
name from the area with which he was most often associated.
This can sometimes be confusing. For example, the small spitz-
type Shikoku and the Tosa, a huge mastiff-like fighting dog,
were both associated with the Island of Shikoku, located in
Kochi Prefecture. Researchers are understandably confused
because the two very dissimilar types were both known as
Shikoku-Kochi.

Fortunately for Westerners struggling to understand
Japanese terminology, the Tosa became a more distinct type
with a specific use and was renamed. The Akita's development
is associated with Akita Prefecture in the northern part of
Japan. More specifically, the breed is closely connected to a
particular town called Odate City,
In repose this is The Claim also known as "Dog City" and
Jumper O'BJ...the Akita is "Boulevard of Dogs."
a lot of "inu" for anyone. Odate City is remotely situated,

10

Am-Can. Ch. Matsutake's Cody Bear Paw, a highly acclaimed sire owned by Canadian breeder Beverly Wilkinson.

surrounded by towering mountain ranges, and virtually shut off to winter travel by severe weather. As was seldom the case with other Oriental breeds, the development of the local dog which was to become the Akita-inu evolved for several hundred years without much infiltration by other developing types and certainly without early European influence. The large region that includes Akita Prefecture remained isolated until the 14th century. In fact, the Hokkaido region is still occasionally referred to as the Ezo-chi or Land of the Ainus.

The influence of Chinese dogs, predominantly of "Chow Chow" type, cannot be denied. Please understand that the magnificent Chow as seen in show rings today bears little resemblance to the ancient dog of China. Old wounds do not heal quickly and following the trouncing by China, the genetic influence of various Chinese breeds was downplayed for obvious reasons. Nonetheless, history cannot be denied and dogs know no political boundaries. Before it was convenient to forget certain details, important writings document that dogs were brought into Japan from China and Korea under the reign of Emperor Jinmu, about 660 BC. The Japanese Chin bears a striking resemblance to the Chinese Temple Dog. *The Observer's Book Of Dogs* (C. Hubbard, 1966) describes the Chinese Coolie Dog as a cross between the "Akita and the Chow Chow, of definite Spitz type..." and although the weight was only about 45 pounds, the color was white with lemon or biscuit markings on the head. Significantly, the description of "ears pendant; tail sickle-shaped" may indicate an Akita more on the order of the Tosa. Pinto coloration, particularly black and white, may trace back to several non-spitz types including the Chinese Karainu and even the smaller Chinese breeds such as the Pekingese. Photographs taken during the early 1900s depict black pinto Akitas, and scrolls from the early Kamakura period (1185-1333) include pinto dogs of Akita type in the background.

With the introduction of Christianity in the 15th century, dogs of every variety began to arrive in Japan along with their European owners. The mastiff influence is still seen today in dogs with an excess of loose skin that may result in hanging ears. The Elkhound and Keeshond-type dogs of true Nordic origin also left their mark on the native dog that the world would come to know as the Akita. The Chinese wolf/Chow Chow influence remained strong even as the primitive Ainu-type dogs began to be diluted by the blood of European dogs. If one were to compare photographs of the early Chow Chows exported to England, the similarity to some Japanese Akitas of the same period is more than uncanny—it's really quite understandable.

The Ainu-type dog was once known as the Matagi-inu, a

Tamara Warren with Ch. O'BJ BigSon's Jake, who was well received by the judges and became a champion in only three shows!

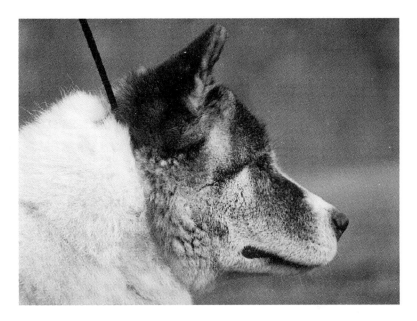

Few Akitas have ever lived up to the record of Ch. O'BJ BigSon of Sachmo, an all-time top winner and sire bred by the author.

word meaning "hunter." The native red dog had light facial markings and coloration common to primitive canines all over the world including the Australian Dingo. The Matagi-inu or Ainu-type was eventually diluted by exposure to the European imports and the inevitable crossbreeding that resulted. Even so, the primitive color pattern remains today and has experienced a resurgence of popularity in Japan, possibly because it is a color combination "foreign" to the breeds that diluted native type. The light face, throat, underbelly, breechings, and paws in combination with solid red body color is seen in other AKC breeds such as the Chow Chow, Shiba, and Finnish Spitz.

We in America can say with pride that the Akita is a wonderful combination of the best of Asian and European dogs. The Japanese have gone to great lengths to breed out all signs of Western influence and, in fact, have been largely successful. The Akita in today's Japan bears little resemblance to the dogs that were brought back to America in the 1940s. Here, we love the fact that the Akita is one of only a very few AKC registered breeds which allows all colors, even though this clearly shows the diversity of his interesting background. Japan is hardly thrilled by evidence of genetic impurity and many of the colors which were once highly favored in Japan are now forbidden! Also culturally displeasing are black dogs with white boots and vest, traditional funeral attire. None of this really matters to us because pinto, black masks, indeed even black tuxedo dogs afford Westerners an infinite palette from which to choose their best friend.

An Akita in solid white was frowned upon until Am-Can. Ch. Kakwa's Orca made a huge splash at the Westminster Kennel Club. The author proudly handled him to many other great wins.

Breed history in Japan and the Western world glows with accounts of courage and loyalty. Akitas were at one time owned only by Japanese royalty. During Emperor Senka's reign, the office of Dog Keeper was officially established and there was a special language used when talking to or about an Akita; the words were actually called "dog words." Care and training of the Akita were very ritualized, even to the various leashes that were used to denote rank and the special manner that was used to tie them up. Dogs achieved rank according to their degree of training and, of course, the personal preference of the Emperor.

The Akita most favored in the Western world is possessive of family and territory, one which not only displays strong guarding instincts but has the boldness to bite if his "pack" is threatened. Although a dog with a strong sense of self is still considered important in Japan, guarding instinct is not. The Japanese still favor a brave fighting spirit while most Americans would just as soon their Akita remembered a little more of his Chow background and was

An appealing 11-week-old puppy, this is Kobun's Soboku the Fire Dancer owned by Mike and Laurie Shanen, bred by Ben and Melonie Herrera.

less aggressive toward other dogs. At first glance, the modern Japanese Akita-inu seems to be a large version of the Shiba, the smallest Japanese dog and one which is rapidly gaining in popularity in the US. Both are clever and determined hunters, both are of spitz type, and both breeds have a notable absence of guarding instinct.

Although Japanese breeders tend to avoid the issue of long-coated Akitas, they do prefer a much heavier coated dog than is usually found in other countries. In America, we have not been successful in eradicating the long coat gene, and, indeed, many owners prefer the profusely coated dogs. The longer coats were probably introduced through both the Chinese Chow and the Russian-type dog known as the Karafuto.

Hokkaido is separated from the former Russian island of Sakhalin by only a narrow channel and when the island became Japanese territory, many young men from the Akita and Aomori areas crossed the strait to Karafuto. The long-coated Akita displays many characteristics once attributed to the believed-to-be-extinct Karafuto dog. They are a bit more laid back, and are generally more obedient and eager to please. Oddly, these characteristics are also found in types that still exist along the Mongolia-Russia border and in China where, depending on dialect, they may be called Foo Dogs. Like the shorter coated dogs, long-coated Akitas are atypical of either the true Arctic type or the Chow Chow. In fact, it's difficult to smoothly fit the Akita breed into either the Arctic breeds or wolf-spitz category. He is quite unique in that he has the best characteristics of both.

The Chinese Foo Dog, a newly revived ancient breed whose newfound popularity and limitless appeal can also be credited to the author. This teddy doll is "Daniel."

In about 1919, Japan established natural monument legislation, designed to preserve culturally significant objects and animals. By 1927 the Akiho (Akita-inu Hozankai) Society was established in Odate City; Nippo (Nippo-kin Hozankai) followed in 1928; and the Akita-inu Akikyo in 1948. Each of these organizations was determined to restore the Akita as a natural monument.

The term Akita-inu was not formally used until 1931 when the breed was finally designated a natural monument. This momentous event was followed in 1934 by the first Japanese dog standard that listed the Akita Dog and subsequently by the Akiho Standard of 1938. There have since been many, many versions and revisions of the Akita breed standard.

Ch. O'BJ Kudos for Kolor shamelessly shows off her head markings.

At just five months of age, this future top-ranked bitch is Ch. Daijobu's Nichiko, bred and owned by Charles and Catherine Bell.

The Akita breed came to signify health and prosperity. Whereas we take flowers to a friend in the hospital, in Japan the patient was as likely to be presented with a small statue of the Akita-inu.

World War II almost destroyed the breed type restoration effort. As families were ripped apart, dogs drifted to the streets where they bred freely in spite of the perils. It was considered traitorous to waste food on a dog, and the luxuriant pelt of the largest Japanese breed was felt to be more useful on a soldier than on an Akita. Ironically, the breed may actually have been saved by American military personnel who began to care for the few remaining dogs, most of them strays. Even as Japan began to recover and think about its great loss of cultural treasures, servicemen returned to the States with dogs they refused to part with.

These "Akitas" were not selected due to any adherence to or concern for type but because of their appeal as individual dogs. No doubt their courage and loyalty spoke to the same virtues in our brave fighting forces.

Still extremely rare, the Akita moved into the AKC Miscellaneous Class in 1955. By 1956 an Akita Club was forming and by 1959 the Akita Club of America came into formal existence. There followed many years of divisiveness, with various clubs and individual owners struggling to become the dominant authority on Akitas. It has been said that most Akita people exhibit the same bold and dominant traits as their dogs! The political fighting and proliferation of splinter clubs were not resolved until the close of 1972 when the AKC approved the Akita standard as presented by the victorious Akita Club of America. That there were many deviations from the various Japanese versions was by then of little consequence. The breed had become Americanized and the AKC dropped the country of origin as is its custom, thus the Japanese Akita became simply the Akita. Today there is a chance the breed will be renamed the American Akita, as has been done in Mexico. This would split the breed into two, such as was the case with the American and English Cocker Spaniels.

Imports continued to be registered as foundation stock until February 1974. The gene pool that established the breed in this country is said to have been very small, consisting of little more than a hundred pedigrees. Others believe that nothing could be further from the truth due to the obvious fact that few of the original dogs brought back from Japan were of pure parentage. Dogs that survived the effects of the war were often turned into the streets by owners who loved them too much to destroy them but could not risk being identified as owners of such large, hungry dogs. Photographs of subsequent generations show the results. Indeed, the Akita that stole the great Helen Keller's heart and with which she was frequently photographed would not today be regarded as purebred in either America or Japan. Still, those early imports had the intelligence and the character that make the breed so great today.

This brindle Nipponese beauty is Kobun's Kiri-Go owned by the Herreras and Carlo Warren.

Registration of Akitas or any other Japanese breed was cut off until April 1992 when the AKC finally recognized the Japanese Kennel Club. One reason the AKC steadfastly refused to honor Japanese export pedigrees was concern for the authenticity of the paperwork and the purity of breeds.

Recognition of the JKC brought great excitement in some quarters. As imports had previously been unregisterable, breeders awaited the anticipated flood of imports from Japan. Such has not been the case although some exquisite dogs have arrived in America, one of which was Winners Bitch at the 1992 National Specialty.

Appearance and behavior are quite different between Japanese and American Akitas. The Japanese have emphasized native type and Oriental features. This has resulted in a wide gap between the best of the lighter boned, smaller, more plushly coated, exquisitely beautiful imports and the substantially larger, stronger, heavier proportioned and shorter coated American Akitas.

The Akita fancy remains divided into three factions: those who would keep the two distinct types separate, those who feel that each type could benefit from blending certain virtues of the other, and those who wish the foreign dogs would all go home! Well, it was diversity of color, size, breed, history, country, and idealism that were the basis for this marvelous breed (and the great melting pot we call America), so some of us smile as we realize that nothing has changed.

Ch. Ruffian Rose O'BJ owned by Debbie Lynch. A closely inbred Akita like this one proves that intelligently planned breedings can create a great dog.

HACHI-KO

Certainly Hachi-Ko is not the only devoted dog the world has known. But his story is, without doubt, one of the most famous in that so many countries shared in Japan's tribute to man's best friend. There are breeds of more ancient history, breeds with a more genetically pure background, and many breeds that have an equally fascinating past. There is, however, no breed possessed of more character, loyalty, and cultural significance than the Akita dog.

Lassie and Rin Tin Tin's world-wide fame couldn't compare to that of the Akita known simply as Hachi-Ko. The big fawn dog was a familiar figure at Shibuya station. His owner, Professor Uneo, commuted daily to his position at Tokyo University and Hachi-Ko escorted him to the train station every morning, returning each evening to meet his beloved master.

Most commuters took the dog's daily presence for granted; however, when his master suffered a heart attack in May 1925, everyone was saddened by the sight of the faithful dog. No doubt, many wished for a way to tell the dog that his master

Ch. Beoth's Three Toes Griz owned by Dave and Lee Ana Dorsett. The nobility and devotion of the Akita can be observed in the expression and stance of a champion.

would never again arrive on the train. Every day, the big Akita met the train and watched hopefully as the passengers emerged from it. Everyone took pity on the dog as he grew thin and ever more depressed.

Commuters brought food and the station master provided a soft bed, but Hachi-Ko took no comfort in their attentions. Professor Uneo's former gardener took the dog in but it was not Hachi-Ko's home. Gradually he began to spend more and more time at the station. Dr. Itagaki, a veterinarian and good friend of Professor Uneo, provided medical attention as required. Hachi-Ko grew older.

By 1932 the press had picked up his story and a bronze statue was commissioned in honor of his fidelity. The Society for the Preservation of Japanese Dogs unveiled the statue in April of 1934. Shibuya Station commuters and onlookers were

emotionally gratified but the old dog was not. He died the
following year at age 11, not old for an Akita, but Hachi-Ko was
aged and lonely for too many years.

When the war broke out a decade later, the huge bronze
statue was melted down and converted into munitions and the
area where it had stood was leveled by bombing raids. When
the war ended, the courage and loyalty of Hachi-Ko became
somewhat of a national symbol. One of the reconstruction
projects became the restoration of the statue in Shibuya
Square. School children in the States, in Japan, and in several
other countries saved their coins and wrote letters about the
famous dog. Even adults responded with letters and stories of
loyal dogs they had known, and they too sent money. Little by
little, the funds were raised. The son of the original sculptor
was located and he agreed to erect a new statue of Hachi-Ko.
Commuters approved. The world was still saddened over the
tragedy of war but somehow the fact that Hachi-Ko was "home
again" brought some measure of reassurance that all would be
right with the world.

The watchful statue became a meeting place for
businessmen and a significant place for lovers. It was, in fact,
young students of Tokyo University who finally realized that
something wasn't quite right. There was one more thing that
must be done to ensure that Hachi-Ko might finally be at
peace. In 1983, the students carried a bust of Professor Uneo
from the school and placed it next to the statue of Hachi-Ko.
Man and dog were finally reunited and in the respectful and
simple ceremony, a story of undying loyalty received a
postscript. Hachi-Ko was happy once again.

*Ch. The
Midnight Torch
O'BJ at seven
months stands
proud and
strong as an
Akita must.*

THE AKITA IN AMERICA

Until the early 80s, the Akita was inconsistent in type, personality, size, and disposition. Certain characteristics have, however, remained consistent in America.

The determination to dominate other dogs and the physical ability to enforce that dominance are coupled with an inherent devotion to family and the physical power to protect his loved ones. These characteristics have been valued from the time the caveman first tossed a bone to

A unique statue from Japan awarded to the author's first great Akita Ch. Okii Yubi's Sachmo of Makoto by famous Japanese judge Mr. Ito. Owned by Bill and Barbara Andrews.

a dark shadow just beyond the glow of the campfire. Our appreciation for such a dog took yet another step when the first Akita, a large male named Taro, was brought into America by a military officer.

Little by little, the Akita breed became scattered across the country. The Hulls settled in Tucson with a pair that produced several litters, and Ted Brinks, director of the San Diego Humane Society, also owned a pair. Dr. Greenlees in New York State had a white female that produced puppies.

The Shaeffers, kennel name "Kensha," in Nebraska, the O'Sheas from Pennsylvania, and the Kams of California were among the first to breed seriously. That these dogs were of varying type and represented a confusing blend of Japanese and European dogs is an undisputed fact, but cognizant Akita owners of today understand that it was that very diversity that prevented the breed from dying on the vine of massive inbreeding. The crossbreeding before (and after) the Akita arrived on American shores ensured survival of a relatively healthy and hardy canine.

Little by little, the gene pool was refined and dominant dogs led to the development of prominent lines. Issei Riki Oji Go, a dominant sire for the O'Sheas, was bred to Kuma's Akai Kosho-Go, a foundation bitch for Sam and Barbara Mullen. This mating produced Ch. Mitsu Kuma's O'Kashihime-go, Mitsu Kuma's Splashdown (Sachmo's granddam) and the breed's first Group winner, Ch. Mitsu Kuma's Tora Oji Go, owned by Terry Wright. The Mullens' New Jersey based Mitsu Kuma Kennels became well known for its contributions.

The Frerose Kennels of Fred Duane were founded on top show dog and producer, AmCanBerm. Ch. Kenjiko Royal Tenji, ROMXP. "Jojo," as he was called, was the grandson of Japanese import Teddy Bear of Toyohashi Seiko.

Import Gyokushu of Tojo Kensha was the grandsire of Krug's Sotto and Michiko of Kensha. Sotto became a foundation sire for Bettye and Francis Krug of Maryland and Michiko a top producer for the Sakura Kennels of Barbara Miller. Ch. Krug's Ichiban Akemi-Go was also the top winning Akita bitch prior to AKC recognition.

In 1971, Barbara Miller had the unusual distinction of owning three generations of obedience titled dogs! At that time, obedience was the only "class" in which Akitas could compete with AKC registered breeds. Those three titled dogs, Prince Jo, CD, his son, Ch. Sakura's Bushi, CD, and his son, Krug's Sachi, CD, owned by the Aigners in Long Island, did much to dispel the breed's reputation as being difficult to work in obedience. The Sakura Kennels also had great breeding success with Prince Jo, a Krug's Sotto son. Prince Jo produced Chujitsu, a foundation bitch for the Okii Yubi Kennels of Robert Campbell, so it's easy to see how the East Coast lines were strongly intertwined.

Bob Campbell shipped Namesu-Joo, a Haru Hime daughter, back to the West Coast to be bred to the mighty Ashibaya Kuma, owned by Bea Hunt. That mating produced Yukan No Okii Yubi, ROMP, who sired Ch. Okii Yubi's Dragon House Ko-

Ch. Hots Melvin O wins the Stud Dog class with his daughters, Ch. Hots Ying-Yang and Ch. Hots Believe It or Not (both out of Ch. Frerose's Annie). Owned by Stephanie Olsen.

Go, ROMXP, owned by the Andrews. Ko-Go was tied as the all-time top-producing dam for over a decade. Bob bred many top-producers including the number one sire of all Working Group dogs, Ch. Okii Yubi's Sachmo of Makoto, ROMXP, also owned by Bill and Barbara Andrews.

This is Ch. Okii Yubi Sachmo of Makoto, the most important Akita ever bred in the United States.

Jap. Gr. Ch. Kumazakura-Go was the grandsire of Oshio's Mako-Go who sired the red pinto Ch. Oshio's Taisho-Go. Traces of Oshio (from Long Beach, CA) are still to be found in a few old dogs such as Ch. Tschumi's Flash. Descending in yet another direction, Kumazakura-Go sired Cripple Creek's Thor, grandsire of top producer Ch. Kin Hozan's Toklat, CD and ROM.

From the same line that produced the great Sachmo dog, this is Okii Yubi Yojo.

The dominant bitch Jap. Gr. Ch. Haru Hime produced very well for Barbara Confer when bred to Jap. Gr.

ST OF BREED
RNHUSKER K.C.

An early Best in Specialty Show Akita, this is Mexican Ch. Kinsei Suna Nihon-No Taishi, Sho-Dan, CD, photographed in the late 1960s.

Ch. Teddy Bear of Toyohashi Seiko. Ch. Sakusaku's Tom Cat-Go, ROMP, is just one of the many top winners and Register Of Merit progeny produced by Teddy Bear and Haru Hime. Haru Hime was both the dam and grandam of Ch. Toyo-No Charlie Brown, a handsome brindle owned and shown by Carol Foti. A popular winner, Charlie Brown sired several important litters but was best known for his show ring presence.

Walter Kam brought several Akitas from Japan to found the famous Triple K Kennels in San Gabriel, California. They produced such great dogs as Mx. Ch. Triple K Hayai Taka and

Ch. Triple K Shinya Ningyo, who produced Triple K Miko, the mother of Ashibaya Kuma. Shinya Ningyo was herself a daughter of Jap. Gr. Ch. Kinsho-Go, a son of Jap. Gr. Ch. Kincho-Go Abe. Ch. Triple K Shoyu-Go was sired by Camille's Kanpuzan dog who was bred to Ch. Triple K Chiyo, a granddaughter of both Jap Gr. Ch. Sakurahime and Hayai Taka.

The Akita Tani Kennel of Liz Harrell was founded on two great dogs that traced back to the Kams' original import stock. Akita Tani's Shoyo Go was sired by Jap. Gr. Ch. Kinsho-Go, who was also the sire of Shinya Ningyo. Shoyo Go was successfully bred to two of his half sisters by Kinsho-Go and also back to his dam, Kokoro. As he was already the product of a father-daughter breeding, their litter produced the very inbred dog, Akita Tani's Tatsumaki, ROM.

Akita Tani's Hayashii Kuma winning at Eden Kennel Club in 1968. Photograph courtesy of Liz Harrell.

Barbara and Mac McDougle, kennel name "Gin Gin," bred a dog destined to become one of the first top-winners following AKC recognition. Can. Mx. and CACIB Ch. Gin Gin Haiyaku-Go of Saku Saku, "Chester" as he was known, was sired by Tom Cat, and although Chet became sterile at an early age, he was a top show dog. He was first owned by Joan Linderman (author of *The Complete Akita*) who then sold him to Stephanie Rubenfeld, House of Treasures (HOT), and Sara Kletter. "Chester" was handled by Fran Wasserman of Date Tensha Kennels.

The famous Ch. Okii Yubi's Sachmo of Makoto, ROMXP, blended the best lines from both coasts through his sire Mikado No Kin Hozan, ROMP, and his dam, Mariko No Kin Hozan. He was purchased by Bill and Barbara "BJ" Andrews as an eight-week-old puppy. Although the acquisition was

27

carefully planned and long awaited, neither the Andrews nor Bob Campbell had any inkling of what lay ahead.

BJ owner-handled Sachmo to numerous ring records and guided him through a very selective but illustrious stud career resulting in 101 AKC Champions.

Building on the original three dogs purchased from Bob Campbell, in a very short time, the Andrews had set more show ring records and produced more Champions, Register Of Merits, and top winners than any other two kennels combined.

But the Akita breed has been blessed with many great dogs and dedicated breeders. Thanks to the efforts of other early pioneers such as Stephanie Olsen, Camille Kam, Gus Bell, Mary Echols, Joan Young, Liz Harrell, Bea Hunt, Joan Linderman, Ceil Hoskins, Merry Atkinson, Barbara Miller, and Bettye Krug, ring stars were already beginning to sparkle before Sachmo had been conceived. Some were also

Ch. O'BJ BigSon of Sachmo broke all show ring records for Akitas, competing in the Working Group (before the Group was split into Working and Herding). BigSon is 16 months old in the photo.

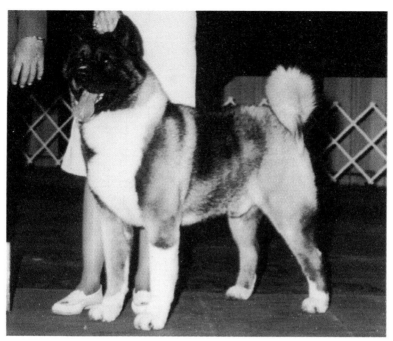

Handled by the author as always, Ch. Okii Yubi's Sachmo of Makoto, ROMXP was ranked in the top five show dogs for five consecutive years. A legendary producer of over 100 champions, Sachmo put the Akita on the map to stay.

beginning to make their genetic prowess felt. Triple K Tomo Go, Fukumoto's Ashibaya Kuma, and Imperial Ginzan were competing with bitches such as Imperial Fuji Hime in specialty matches. The East Coast admired Barbara Miller's Sakura boys, Banjaku and Bushi, as well as Akita Tani's Yoro Kobi No Moto, and lovely females like Krug's Sachi and Krug's KoKo.

By 1980, the breed was a serious contender in Group rings. Easily remembered are Ch. Golden Sun's Tanahea, bred and owned by Merry Wicker; the BIS "Brown Bear"; the Rubenfeld-Kletter star "Chester" competing with his sire Tom Cat; Sachmo competing with his son Jumbo; and, of course, the Frerose ambassador Jojo. Tanahea consistently defeated the males and was in the top spot until Ch. Wanchan's Akagumo, aka "Brown Bear," took his BIS near the close of the year. Ch. Okii Yubi's Sachmo of Makoto had become a standard item in the top ten rankings and the great show dog "Chester" (Ch. Gin Gin Haiyaku-Go Of Saku Saku) began to concede to younger dogs. Ch. Tobe's Peking Jumbo was holding court in the Northeast, and then suddenly a string of top winners began to emerge. Ch. Tamarlane's Silver Star, owned by Dean and Bonnie Hermann, edged out the West Coast male Gaylee's O'Kaminaga; Ch. Orca began to make his mark as the Andrews' Canadian import; Rick Musisca's Ch. Pharfossa's Michael was winning hearts

The legend of The Widow-Maker O'BJ is alive and well. He is the number one owner-handled Akita of all time. This dog was not only a spectacular showman but also the producer of 65 champions.

and ribbons; and Nadine Fontano's big Galloping Gourmet dog attracted a following. Bill and Marcia Erwin turned everyone's applecart upside down when they bought Ch. Mike Truax's Royal Tikara Pal and turned him into a Best in Show winner and top Group contender. The Andrews sold Orca when "the baby" finished from puppy class and, as they were to do again years later with The Widow-Maker, they began to "special" Ch. O'BJ BigSon Of Sachmo before he was dry behind the ears. But before there was any of that, there was Sachmo—the dog who opened so many doors for all the great Akitas that were to follow.

The entire dog world paid attention when the premier dog magazine *Kennel Review* listed him as the Number One Sire of all dogs competing in the Working Group classification. Sachmo had sired only 29 litters and his oldest kids were not even three years old! Even his competitors were proud. After

Am-Can. Ch. Kakwa's Orca, ROMXP shown competing in the Working Group at Westminster Kennel Club in Madison Square Garden. Owned by Bill and Barbara Andrews, handled by Sidney Lamont.

all, he was an Akita, a breed many people would never have given a second thought to were it not for Sachmo's incredible accomplishments. Suddenly, everyone was talking about the "new" breed. Even today, many judges remember "that great Sachmo dog." He did for the Akita breed what Man 'O War did for Thoroughbred horses. Indeed, Sachmo was the king!

Carol Foti made history as the much envied handler of the first Best in Show Akita, Ch. Wanchan's Akagumo, bred and co-owned by Pete Lagus. The judge was Anna Katherine Nicholas, the place was California, and the weather was a scorching 90-plus degrees on hot asphalt! To say that Carol had that dog in condition is indeed an understatement. There is a lesson in the fact that the "Brown Bear's" incredible achievement exceeded his abilities at stud, thus few Akita fanciers today can recall who he was or even who cracked the Best In Show ring for the breed. Everyone with a pedigreed Akita knows names like Sachmo, Widow-Maker, BigSon, Daimyo, and Michael.

Unlike some working breeds, Akita females have often done well in "head to head" ring competition. Ch. Matsu Kaze's Holly Go Lightly, bred by Gus Bell, owned by Bea Hunt, and handled by Rusty Short, made Best in Show history along with Sachmo's half sister Ch. Big A Stormy Of Jobe owned by Gary and Janet Voss.

Owners are equally proud to point out top dams on their pedigrees. Bitches such as Mad Hatter, Sarah Lei, Ko-Go, Jazz, Vampirella, Dietka, Key-Too and Georgia Peach have given the breed over a hundred champions and top producers.

The *Akita Reference* Hall Of Fame list of top breeders added new and important names to the ranks of significant contributors. Judy Bessette, Julie Hoehn, Bonnie Hermann, Vicky Dooms, Linda Hensen, Ed Israel, Ingrid Linerud, Sophia Kaluzniaki, Sara Kletter, Sylvia Thomas, Chris Weatherman, Carol McKulski, and many other dedicated breeders were working hard to improve quality and eliminate genetic faults in a breed that the public was taking to heart.

The first Schutzhund titled Akita was crowned Ch. Charisma's Miko Go No K Mikado. A half brother to Sachmo through Mikado No Kin Hozan, he also attained AKC titles of CDX and UD. His owners/trainers, Steve and Janice Mitchell, may still hold the record for the most titled Akita.

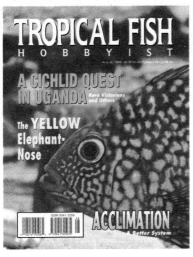

Since 1952, Tropical Fish Hobbyist has been the source of accurate, up-to-the-minute, and fascinating information on every facet of the aquarium hobby. Join the more than 60,000 devoted readers worldwide who wouldn't miss a single issue.

Subscribe right now so you don't miss a single copy!

AKITAS AROUND THE WORLD

Canadian Akitas were developing from mostly American lines and many breeders achieved titles in both countries despite a few differences in the breed standards.

The breed exploded in Great Britain. The first Akita was sent from Canada to Marian Sargent with another bitch being imported in 1981 by Gerald and Kath Mitchell. Two more were also imported from Japan, and by 1984, 12 Akitas were registered with the English Kennel Club. The first American Champion sent to England was also the dam of the first litter to be born in Great Britain. Ch. O'BJ Sachette No Okii Yubi, exported to Meg Purnell-Carpenter of the Overhill Kennels by BJ Andrews, whelped a litter in October 1983 sired by another O'BJ import, O'BJ Aces High. Two more litters followed: one bred by Mr. and Mrs. Mitchell of Kiskas Kennels born November 1983 out of Kosho Ki KiKi, and then in December 1983 Beryl Mason's bitch Yukihimi-Go produced a litter.

BJ Andrews went to the

The first Akita to win a Best in Show is the claim to fame of Ch. Wanchan's Akagumo, known as Brownie. Bred by Dr. and Mrs. P. Lagus, Brownie was an exceptional mover and a great show dog.

1985 Crufts show in England, the largest show in the world, and handled Overhill's Lizzy's Girl to Best of Breed Any Variety NSC, the first Akita to win this top honor and, certainly, the first American Akita to do so. It was all the more to Meg Purnell-Carpenter as Lizzy's Girl was from that first British-born litter. Lizzy and her litter sisters, Overhill's Marlow's Miracle and Overhill's Kita Mori, were all successful show dogs and producers.

The first official breed classes for Akitas were topped by another Andrews export, The Steel Glove O'BJ. The breed was on its way and by 1990 over 600 Akitas were registered with The Kennel Club. By 1995 it was estimated that there were as many as 4000.

The first Challenge Certificates were awarded at the 1990 Crufts show to Sophia Kaluzniacki's Am. Ch. Tamarlane's Veni Vidi Vici, shown in England by Mike Window. The bitch Challenge Certificate went to Kiskas Jezebel. Am. Ch. Tamarlane's Veni Vidi Vici completed his mission, becoming the first English Champion before returning home to the States to claim Best Veteran at the National Specialty.

Mexico has always welcomed the California crowd but in 1989 an Akita made a lot of Mexican owners unhappy by becoming the Number One Dog of All Breeds! This spectacular red pinto was AmMx. Int'l. Ch. O'BJ Sachmo Ko-Son by Ch. O'BJ BigSon Of Sachmo, owned by Jorge Haddad, Jr.

Soon all of the Americas fell in love with the Akita and there have been quite a number of top winners throughout Central and South America. The Akitas Ace program of Maurizio Moretto in Chile has garnered several Best in Show wins.

Meg Purnell-Carpenter's Overhill Kennels in England continues to produce the best Akitas in Great Britain. This promising youngster is Takehiro at six months of age.

Maurizio also enjoys the proud distinction of importing what was to become the first female Group Winner, Ch. The One-To-Keep O'BJ. Mr. Moretto also imported a double Widow-Maker grandson, a black-faced, black dog with white stockings. Thunderhawk O'BJ enjoyed tremendous success in Chile but more importantly, amid the "repositioning" of several prominent breeders due to the "ban" on such colors in JKC and FCI shows, Thunderhawk went to the largest international show of all, the World Show in Buenos Aires, and there he swept the breed rings every day!

Overhill's Pacer is a lovely brindle import from Meg Purnell-Carpenter.

Luis Cincunequi of Guatemala City, Central America, has also had excellent success in Mexico and the Americas. Competing in both FCI and "regular" shows, his two O'BJ dogs, one black-masked and the other self-masked brindle, have done equally well. The Jucep Kennels of Dr. Parra in Columbia have also had tremendous interbreed success with the big black pinto Ch. "Ziggy."

The breed gained great popularity in Australia following the first American import, Australian Ch. and BIS winner O'BJ Piece Of The Rock owned by Ken Taylor. Many other great Akitas followed and strong bloodlines have developed in the vast land "down under."

As popularity grows in the States and in other countries, health and temperament must be of primary concern. The character of a proud and dominant breed must not be eroded by those who desire a more "saleable" product. The Akita is not suitable for every family. That is no discredit to either the dog or the prospective owner. The delightfully busy Shiba, the distinguished but somewhat klutzy Wolfhound, the inscrutable Chow Chow, the happy, easygoing Golden Retriever, or the sturdy but dominant little Corgi—all have specific personality and character traits that appeal to one family but not another. We must not attempt to change the Akita into some "other" breed or he will be forever lost to those who appreciate a dignified, brave, and innately unique guard-companion.

OWNING An Akita

So what does all this history mean to you, the prospective owner? Loyalty is just one of the characteristics that is so much a part of the Akita. Some would say stubbornness is also typical. I prefer not to think of the breed as stubborn but as independent and single-minded. When the Akita sets his mind to something, he is more likely to achieve it than is the average dog.

If the goal is to escape from your yard or from the car, sooner or later your Akita will succeed. However, typical of the breed, he probably won't go anywhere except to find you. If you're in the house, he will likely go to the door and announce that the "yard" is not where he wants to be. Akitas like shopping excursions but are not always fond of being left in the car. One dog was known to check each store entrance until he discovered which one his owner had entered. He would then pass time in inventive ways, the best of which was nosing everyone's posterior as they passed by his post. Fortunately, he lived in a small town with indulgent citizens and slow traffic. The owner eventually convinced the young dog that guarding her car was his job, whereupon he never again abandoned the vehicle. Personally, I suspect it was his embarrassment at being fooled when she began to frequent a newly opened mall, going in one department store only to emerge a block away....

Akitas are especially clever at figuring out situations, problems, puzzles, and what's inside the refrigerator! Can dogs reason? Some authorities say no. Can

The Akita, like its miniature Japanese cousin the Shiba, can be counted among the brightest of dogs, if not the most trainable. As for all spitz breeds, fences are imperative!

Though nobility and affection don't often travel in like circles, Akitas can be "licky" as demonstratively demonstrated by kisser Int. Ch. Target Rose O'BJ and kissee Maurizo Moretto.

Akitas reason? This authority says emphatically, yes!

A young Widow-Maker son owned by the Allens learned where the coldest water was kept. While the average Akita will settle for a few gulps from the freshly flushed commode bowl, Ch. Ringer thought otherwise. Repeatedly confronted by a large puddle in front of the refrigerator and absolutely certain there was no leaky pipe, Richard Allen set his video camera on a tripod and the family settled down in the living room. An hour or so later, Ringer yawned, got up, and headed for the kitchen. A scant two minutes later he returned, sighed, and laid back down by Sally Jo.

Richard retrieved the camera, rewound the tape, and later shared it with us. The inanimate scene became interesting as the big dog entered the kitchen and took note of the camera. He seemed suspicious; but after almost fogging up the lens, he eased over to the refrigerator just like a child about to snitch a cookie. He stood quietly, cocking his head to listen for

This Akita and his young travel companion are ready for the high road. Owner, Meg Purnell-Carpenter. footsteps. Then he reared up, placed a huge paw on the lever of the ice water dispenser and pushed—just like you or I would do! He lapped the icy water, dropped back to all fours, stepped closer to the doorway, quite obviously listened again, and then, satisfied he was undetected, smoothly re-executed the complicated maneuver. The precise and deliberate way in which he repeated his previous actions dispelled any doubt that he had accidentally placed his paw on the vertical lever in just the right way, applied just the right amount of pressure, and held the lever back with his footpad in order to drink—actually a rather awkward feat.

Can Akitas reason? Case closed.

Some trainers characterize the breed as stubborn or, even more indicative of their lack of credentials, as "untrainable." Nothing could be further from the truth. In fact, the Akita is like a precocious child who does not learn by rote but who instead wants to know the why and wherefore of everything. This can be as frustrating for an Akita owner as it is for a parent but the rewards are equally interesting.

Let's look at formal obedience training. The Akita is quite likely to want an explanation about why he should go 'round and 'round in circles, stopping every minute or so, wherein he is expected to sit. To further test his powers of reasoning, no sooner does he sit than his human partner wants to go again! Worse than that, his trainer can't seem to decide which way he wants to go. First he turns to the left, then to the right, then

With patience and knowledge of the way an Akita thinks, the breed can be trained for any number of unconventional activities. These well-trained Akitas are leading the parade.

seems to suddenly make up his mind because he takes off running! Akitas are willing to indulge their owners but only up to a point of reason. After about ten minutes, especially if the session is during the heat of the day, a smart Akita is quite likely to plunk his butt down and plainly say "Ah, you go ahead and when you've decided where we're going, come back and get me. In the meantime I'll just sit here and do my best to ignore your confusion." Stubborn? Obviously it depends on one's point of view.

A professional trainer needs to grasp the "Why?" factor and the inherent independence that dictates how the Akita approaches the traditional training session. The breed is programmed to make instantaneous decisions with no human guidance. When dealing with a bear or a canine opponent, a dog is hardly going to appreciate human instructions. If he's bold enough to stand ground, he isn't as likely to bow to regimentation as are some other breeds. Let me put it this way: if the Akita were human, he would be leading a medical team into the rain forest, pushing a jet to its limits, diving to the ocean floor, or riding bulls in a rodeo!

Okay, so there are some troublesome aspects associated with owning an Akita. One is size. To someone cuddling a 15-

pound puppy, the realization that the teddy bear will grow into a grizzly bear of over 100 pounds is pretty remote. He won't fit comfortably in the family car and the vet will not have the psychological advantage of examining him up on the table.

Should I tell you that the luxuriant soft puppy coat will eventually fall out? That's right! It will turn into hair balls, which always hide out under the sofa except when your mother-in-law is knocking at the door. Then they drift out into the middle of the room or float onto the icing of the cake you just prepared.

As a puppy, the Akita is the original teddy bear—even if the breed was once used to hunt bear! Akitas require a dedicated and experienced owner.

Akitas require less food in proportion to their size than do many other breeds. Nonetheless, what goes in must come out. A large size pooper scooper is advised. The good side of the coin is that, like most Oriental breeds, the Akita is exceptionally clean and rarely soils his surroundings.

Akitas do very well in an apartment, as they do not require a tremendous amount of exercise. However, like all dogs, they must eliminate at least four times per day. They should never, ever be "paper trained" unless one is prepared to use the entire *New York Times* Sunday edition several times a day! If given reasonable opportunity to eliminate outside, the Akita will select a spot as far away from the dwelling as is possible, preferably a secluded corner of his fenced yard. Having christened that spot as the bathroom, he will return to it each time. Knowing where his bathroom is located makes the chore of cleaning it much simpler. Apartment owners will soon learn which are the preferred toilet stops along the walking route. Urination will be frequent and happen at the first curb, but owners should note that a certain amount of physical activity is

Ma-Kobe's Yukico O'BJ snoozing away the days of puppyhood. Akitas, despite their size, can do quite well in the city and suburbs as they don't need as much exercise as some other large breeds.

Although Akitas do well in single-dog homes, with proper introduction and acclimation they can accept other dogs as friends. This Akita and Miniature Bull Terrier puppy seem to have a lot in common.

required in order to effectively move the bowels. Thus a brisk walk or jog will bring "results" quicker than will a leisurely stroll.

Frequently asked questions deserve knowledgeable, truthful answers, not sales hype or idealistic fantasy. There are two breed characteristics that must be discussed with emphasis and complete candor.

Akitas are guard dogs. They have an inherent ability to protect their home territory, possessions, and loved ones. Their possessive-protective instincts have been fine-tuned for many generations. If one is not prepared to accept the responsibility of owning a dog that will bite to protect, then by all means, one should choose a breed that does not have these traits.

There is a shocking difference between the idealistic concept of a big, powerful friend who would kill for you and the reality of owning an animal who has that capacity. It may be comical when a tiny lap dog barks and snaps at a hand extended toward his loved one. It is decidedly unfunny (and out of character) when it's a one-hundred-pound Akita. While we've established that dogs do "think," they are largely controlled by instinct, that mysterious code which is embedded in every cell and which many believe may even be a link to genetic memory. When indulgent owners fail to comprehend rules of canine discipline and pack order, the result is often a snappy, spoiled, dominant-aggressive, legal liability.

We are inveterate inventors. We spend generations developing a breed that will stand by us against all challenges, a dog in which the bite inhibitor genes are *unmodified* so that he will, in fact, lock those powerful jaws on a human being. We must then be equally capable teachers, instructing owners on the basics of canine behavior and responsible ownership. One need not be physically strong to be a good Akita owner but one must be assertive and authoritative. An indulgent owner who fails to enforce discipline will do better with a smaller breed of softer personality.

Gris Gris is a "champion" to his young girl friend and his owners, Drs. Jon and Cindy Strohmeyer.

The second characteristic that many owners find downright unhandy has to do with the breed's desire to dominate other dogs. The breed standard uses the term "aggressive," which implies that the Akita is rather terrier-like or scrappy. Not so. He will fight at the drop of a hat, the bell for round one, or, as is more often the case, when unknowingly encouraged by his owner! For example, reel a dog in and hold him by the collar, all the while murmuring "good boy, good boy, it's all right" as another dog approaches stiff-legged and wary. Or worse yet, do so as you warn a child to "stay away, he might bite." What have you done? In the first case, you've praised the dog for aggressive behavior exacerbated by being tightly held and feeling the sensation of pressure about his neck. Of course you mean "good boy" because he's still by your side but to him it means that it's good that his blood is heating up at the approach of the strange dog. In the second instance, your reassuring "it's all right" translates into "go get 'em" to the confused animal!

Please, this is not an exaggeration. Misguided owners behave exactly this way over and over again, each time instilling the worst possible behavior pattern in the dog. Re-read the previous paragraph, think about the various ways in which it applies, and then never forget it! If you choose any dog of the Working Group classification, make sure you also select a qualified person to help you with the basics, preferably someone who owns a well-mannered, well-adjusted dog of a guarding breed. It may be an obedience instructor, a professional handler, or a breeder.

While the male Akita will allow a certain degree of "hen-pecking," he is usually the boss and the female dog knows how far she can go. He will not tolerate any other male dog in a less than subservient role. Is the same true for females? Yes. Will the Akita get along with other dogs if it is well trained? The answer is, the dog will be more socially polite and hopefully under better control but training will not change its genetic makeup. Ask any trainer how impossible it is to keep a Basset Hound from sniffing or a gundog from alerting to the flutter of wings.

OK. Next question. Won't "good breeding" eliminate the aggressive attitude or the desire to dominate? Excuse me. Good breeding is what put the attitude into the Akita! It's the arrogance, the dominance, the dignity, the "king of dogs" attitude that attracted you to the Akita to begin with, right? Dominant, by the way, does not mean "bully." Good breeding and attention to detail is what makes a purebred dog generally superior to a mutt and always a more predictable choice. Breeding selectivity enables a Greyhound to run faster than a Bloodhound. It makes a Clumber Spaniel an excellent hunter and a sweetheart companion. And it makes the Akita a confident, dominant, courageous, protective family dog.

Another common misconception is that neutering somehow changes the Akita's genetic programming. Money hungry breeders (or poorly informed trainers and vets) have been known to assure prospective owners that a neutered Akita will take on the personality of a Cocker Spaniel. Full castration (not the newest veterinary gimmick, a vasectomy) will definitely stop the production of testosterone. Castration turns a stallion, generally not the best pleasure or performance mount, into an attentive, dependable steed. It works the same way in dogs. He becomes much more tuned in to the family, and his duties as a companion watchdog remain uppermost in his thoughts. He's no longer frustrated by the enticing scent of the female in season down the street. If you didn't know why he so often seemed moody or distracted, that's because you did not know what he knew....

The breed is hardy enough to sleep outdoors, though he would much rather be inside near his family.

Does castration mean he will live in harmony with another dominant male dog? Does it mean he'll go for a romp in the park with his arch-enemy? C'mon, you know the answers. If, in fact, surgical sterilization so altered his basic personality that he would become a subservient Akita, would you still respect him? Would he still be the canine hero you fell in love with? You are the only one who can answer that question. My emphatic suggestion is to buy a second dog of the opposite sex or to add a submissive happy-go-lucky breed as a new family member. Get a cat. Akitas are so cat-like that they accept the quiet company of a feline as long as it belongs to them. Woe be unto the neighbor's cat that strays into your yard.... And please, extrapolate everything I've said to include female Akitas. Spare yourself the emotional turmoil that always ends in heartbreak. I know hundreds of breeders and owners who have tried to make it work but can cite only one situation wherein two unaltered adult Akitas of the same sex lived together without at some point engaging in mortal combat. Those are the odds with which every experienced, honest breeder will agree.

THE AKITA AS A FAMILY PET

The Akita is "fierce as a Samurai, gentle as a kitten." I've described the female as an "iron hand in a velvet glove" and so she is. Gentle, openly affectionate, quite like the female of most species, she's programmed to care for and nurture the young. She's especially happy if that includes human young and is therefore more inclined to be dressed in doll clothes and ridden in a wagon than is the male Akita. I mean really! Can the male dog maintain that awesome dignity while wearing a pair of sunglasses and dad's old hunting cap?

That is not to say that the male Akita will not be extremely protective of and an excellent companion for his family's children. Just as the king of beasts will roll over and tolerate having his ears bitten by cubs of his own pride, so too will the male Akita stretch out on the floor and let the children use him as a TV pillow. But one must remember that even the lioness may not be so tolerant of another female's cubs and so it is with dogs and the young of another "pack."

Akitas and cats can get on so well it's uncanny.... the cat must "belong" to the Akita. Strange cats are never welcome—you must socialize the puppy and cat so that he accepts the cat as his own. Owner, John Seaborn.

Puppies will accept children as members of their "pack." Akita puppies look for a leader, and this alpha toddler is taking her Akita playmate to a shady retreat.

If your Akita grew up with youngsters running in and out of the house along with the exuberant squealing and mock fights that occur between rambunctious children, so much the better. If you don't have children but want a fully socialized, well-rounded adult dog, then you must take the time (while he's a puppy) to introduce him to well-behaved youngsters. Take him to parks, playgrounds, and softball fields where children play under the supervision of their parents. Be sure to take along treats that he likes, such as tiny tidbits of food that you can secretly hand to the children so they can "feed the doggie," thereby establishing a friendly anticipation when your puppy meets children. Above all, **never** subject your Akita to any manner of teasing or oppressive "smothering" by intense children—even if they're your boss's ill mannered kids. Remember the analogy to the pack or pride. No matter how well you have socialized your dog, he may not be so tolerant of strange children, especially if they become unruly or seem to threaten *his* children. How can your dog be expected to understand that Cousin Johnny isn't really hurting six-year-old Susie? When Johnny chases her with his toy gun and she squeals for help, your protective Akita may try to do just that! Instinct may take over, in which case he will try to stop the perceived attack by disciplining the unruly and annoying "puppy."

Additionally, other children may not have been taught respect for animals and they may not understand that animals suffer pain. They may have only a stuffed toy, thus their experience is limited to the fantasy of television. Youngsters dare each other and get into trouble; better it isn't with your family pet.

You should also understand that grabbing a puppy by the head or neck, pinning it to the ground, and growling softly is a perfectly natural form of canine discipline. Mother dogs do it with their babies every day. The pup understands, immediately goes limp, and sometimes urinates as a sign of submission. The problem is that humans interpret that same action as an assault with the result being a panicked reaction. We can't help it. Our instincts are just as deeply ingrained and defined as those of the now-domesticated canine. Our genetically programmed fear of the wolf-predator combines with the sort of

Akitas, when properly socialized and trained, will allow toddlers to climb on them and ride them. Supervision is essential in every case. Akitas will eventually tire of rough play and seek relief or escape.

instantaneous reaction that often saves an antelope from the fang. So, the child screams and tries to get away instead of going submissively limp like a puppy, parents or onlookers react like humans are supposed to, and in the blink of an eye all that can go wrong has, with the inevitable result that another dog-bites-child statistic is logged.

Akitas are powerful animals, and animals deserve respect and kind handling.

Please do not misunderstand. I am no more defending the canine than am I suggesting that a mother should quietly sip tea as a predator pounces on her offspring. My purpose is to stress how important it is, no matter which breed you select, to take the time to develop a socially conditioned, well-mannered, and obedient dog. The biggest, the first, and the most important rule: **never leave small children alone with a dog.** Would you leave them to play unsupervised in a construction site? Whether it's a small dog that the child may injure or a giant of the dog world

Ch. Okii Yubi's Dragon House Ko-Go, a famous dog bred by Robert Campbell, loved puppies. Here she is greeting her nine-week-old grandson.

that can hurt a child just by flopping down on him, over 97 percent of all animal bites are the direct result of adult carelessness and the genetically conditioned responses of two very dissimilar species. No matter how irrational the behavior may seem to the other and no matter how well-educated each participant may be, each will react as it always has for thousands of years. Sorry 'bout that. Our deepest fiber screams "run" when we see teeth....

There is one other observation that may put things in pleasing perspective with regard to the family pet. Dogs rarely suffer the same expressions of mental instability as do humans. They don't take psychotic drugs, although (shiver) a growing use of Prozac™ in veterinary medicine has been reported. Simply put, dogs are not by nature criminal, homicidal, or sociopathic. Dogs came to our campfire willingly. They are descendants of the wolf, a species that has a very highly developed social structure, one that is respectful of the elderly and tolerant of the young. It's up to us with our superior intelligence to understand their social code and anticipate their behavior. After all, we brought them into our living rooms; we should take the time to learn how they think and react!

More than most dogs, Akitas still resemble the noble wolf from which they descended. The Akita's natural instincts and social behaviors also portray his lupine beginnings.

Akitas are large, naturally aggressive dogs. No matter how extraordinary your Akita is around children, you should never leave the dog alone with small children. If that's all you learn from this book, you have more than gotten your money's worth!

GROOMING

Some prospective owners are concerned about grooming requirements. Actually, the therapeutic benefits of grooming your dog are many. A quiet half hour spent combing, brushing, and beautifying a dog is a half hour during which the hands are busy, the body is relaxed, and the mind is unfettered by business

Akitas don't require excessive grooming—except when they're "blowing coat." For those times, it pays to acclimate the puppy to the routine.

pressures. It is something every dog and his owner can look forward to, provided the dog has had a certain amount of pre-schooling and preparation.

The dog should learn to stand up on a grooming table or a sturdy wooden picnic table. Begin with brief sessions during which nothing elaborate is attempted—just let the puppy enjoy the sensation of the brush and your hands stroking him. Speak to him, sing, or, if you have nothing good to share with him about your day and you're musically uninclined, just repeat his name frequently, accompanied by "good boy" or a reminder command such as "steady." When it comes to stress reduction, why, grooming is almost as good as the Gregorian Chant!

You'll need the proper tools: a shedding rake, which looks like it sounds—a tiny garden rake with one single row of fixed teeth that penetrate the deep undercoat and gently pull the dead hair out through the guard coat; a good chrome, long-toothed finishing comb with both narrow- and wide-spaced teeth; and a plastic- or wooden-backed grooming brush with flexible metal bristles. Heavy duty toenail clippers made for big dogs are a necessity if your dog is on grass and carpet. You will also need cotton swabs to clean the ears and a spray bottle, the sort used to mist plants, filled with water or grooming spray. Mist the hair as you brush and comb, the object being to prevent breakage of top coat while pulling out dead coat and to add conditioner as you groom.

Always towel dry an Akita. Be efficient and quick. Hair dryers help because a coat left to "air dry" will not appear as clean or well-kept.

Adult house dogs will need bathing only once or twice a year. Puppies, like children, seem to have an affinity for mud puddles so they will need more frequent cleaning or brushing. Bathing too often will dry the skin, compromising the naturally protective barrier of a healthy skin and coat. In bad weather, even an adult may become unavoidably muddy underneath but a quick wash-up of the feet, legs, and underbelly will suffice.

Whether it's an all-over bath or a wash-up, dry the dog as thoroughly and quickly as possible, particularly any white areas as they can turn yellowish if left to dry naturally. A regular hair dryer along with the brush and comb will lift and separate the coat and facilitate the drying process. Don't overlook the armpits, groin, under the neck, and the place that seems never to dry—right where the tail rests on the back. A coat left damp down at the skin during hot summer weather can lead to what is appropriately called "hot spots." These troublesome skin eruptions may require veterinary treatment if not discovered and treated right away—another reason for frequent grooming sessions, especially during seasonal shedding.

Flea shampoos and preparations are rarely needed in a dog with good immunities and healthy skin. While we've never resorted to such products, we do use supplements such as garlic, which not only boosts nutritional value but converts the dog into a distasteful meal for fleas and ticks. The addition of 500 mg of vitamin C and about 200 IU of vitamin E per day will also benefit your Akita.

FEEDING

Today's premium quality dry foods are excellent and, overall, a better balanced formula than most of us could prepare. However, they are no more "complete" than is a particular brand of cereal that claims to be total nutrition. You would not rear your child on nothing but cereal, and you can't raise a healthy dog on only the stuff in a bag.

Oriental buddies, Ch. Windom's the Jazzman and his Tibetan Spaniel friend relax in the shade.

Only a flicker of time ago, the canine consumed fresh fruits, berries, grasses, and roots along with birds, fish, snails, mice, and large game animals. The food was consumed raw and included the intestinal contents of game. I'll say simply that you can measurably add to your dog's overall

Akitas like vegetables. No dog is a pure carnivore. Offer your Akita fresh vegetables—carrots are useful in training too, and Akitas go bananas for them!

health and longevity by including fresh and raw whole foods in his diet. Many Akitas appreciate apples, grapes, or bananas. All dogs relish canned fish and raw beef. Don't risk salmonella—hard boil eggs and chicken. Carrots, broccoli, and green leaf vegetables will be a welcome addition to his diet. A side bonus is that he'll stop eating the grass that he has previously vomited all over your carpet! Cottage cheese and yogurt are excellent natural sources of protein but frankly not "normal" for any adult mammal. If you live in the country, unpasteurized cow's or goat's milk will suit his digestive system better.

SELECTING Your Akita Puppy

Now that you know what the Akita should be, how can you make the best choice for your next best friend? Whether you are interested in a show dog from which to raise a litter or two, or you want a quality family companion, you would be well advised to contact a successful show breeder with longevity in the sport. There are many reasons for this.

First, in order to be successful, the breeder has obeyed certain genetic rules and displayed a responsibility and commitment to the art of producing dogs that are superior in appearance, health, and breed temperament. Dog breeders come in many shapes, sizes, and degrees of honesty and authenticity, so you're better off to go to someone with an established reputation who cares about protecting it. That person will care about your satisfaction but above all else care about the welfare of the living creature he planned, whelped, and nurtured.

The number of people selling "show-quality puppies" that don't even own a show dog, i.e., an AKC or KC Champion, is simply amazing. Common sense tells us we would not buy a Kentucky Derby hopeful from a farmer with two mules, a plow, and a "Thoroughbred colt."

Make sure the seller has verifiable credentials. The Kennel Club publishes a

Ch. St. Elmo's Satsuma Doll O'BJ, bred and owned by Sally Jo Allen, has everything an owner could desire in a show puppy: good size, strong bone, straight legs, triangular eyes and ears, and a correct head.

When selecting from a litter as exceptional as this one bred by Mark Nisbet, you can make no wrong decision. Note the consistency of type, calm dispositions, and alert expressions.

monthly magazine that lists the results of every show in the country, including details about every dog that becomes a Champion Of Record. People who are breeding quality dogs take great pride in referencing those records as proof that their dogs are healthy, sound, beautiful, and of good temperament.

The breeder should be more than willing to give you a guarantee that spells out what you have purchased (quality, price, and replacement terms) but more importantly, you must be satisfied that the breeder is financially capable and morally willing to back up whatever piece of paper he hands you. Someone who is eking out mortgage payments or earning a living from dog breeding is unlikely to be sympathetic to any developmental problems the puppy may encounter and is usually unresponsive to your pleas for help. "After the sale" support is very important, even to an experienced dog owner. The breeder should be not only willing but qualified to guide you through the fun of raising, training, showing, or breeding your Akita.

The pedigree should show that at least one of the parents is a Champion. If in doubt, ask for a copy of the champion certificate; it's easy for the unscrupulous to add a non-existent title when making out a pedigree. If the champions aren't there, don't buy cop-out excuses such as the dog "doesn't like the show ring" or "has won some ribbons" or "will be shown later." Has the mom been shown? More to the point, did she win? Do they have the ribbons to prove it? If the ribbons are any color other than blue or purple, they are meaningless.

What about the sire? If he's not a champion, why would they breed him? Perhaps they didn't want to spend the money to breed a dog certified as above average. Hmmmm. Well, they must not have cared much about what they were doing, right? Were they willing to spend the money to feed the pups well and to provide proper medical care for the babies and the mom? Not likely.

At ten weeks old, this Widow-Maker granddaughter has it all. This is Ch. Atarashi's Trouble-Maker.

The demand for championship titles is not one of snobbery. The absence of proof of quality usually means that the litter owner was not interested enough in what he was doing to be bothered with networking with other dog lovers, learning what makes a dog worth breeding, learning how to avoid genetic defects, and properly raising the litter he's planning, etc. Worse yet, no "Ch." title may indicate more than ignorance or lack of interest on the part of the litter owner. He may know full well that the mother can't be shown or wouldn't win. Perhaps she limps, bites, or is shy. It does make one wonder. If the breeder isn't willing to spend money and time before creating a litter, can that person be expected to spend time after he has your money?

An extraordinary puppy owned by Akitas Ace. Confidence and soundness mingle beautifully in this Best in Show youngster.

Speaking of genetic health, all eight-week-old puppies are adorable. Hip, eye, temperament, orthopedic, immune system, and blood disease—these problems are rarely evident in puppies. You should, however, see puppies that are clean and vibrant, with eyes sparkling. Tummies should be obvious but not bulging unless they've just been fed. They should be chubby with plush and shiny coats, their tails should be cranked up on the back in a curled position, and their ears may or may not be up but they should be thick and fit the head at eight weeks. The feet should be thick and tight. Splayed feet or flat toes are a dead giveaway of poor breeding or health—sometimes both!

The critical imprinting period in the canine is 21 to 28 days. If the litter hasn't been properly socialized during that time, nothing you can do will make a well-adjusted dog out of the uninterested, shy, or fearful puppy. Healthy, well-loved puppies should always be ready for human attention. They won't be quite as playful with full tummies but they will still be glad to see you. They should want to bite your fingers and shoelaces, snuggle close, bounce around, and, in easily understood puppy language, invite you to chase them.

If the pups are brought out one at a time and you're not allowed to see how and where they are kept; if the mother dog is not on premises or is "put away"; or if the place is dirty, the breeder unkempt, or the pups lean or lethargic, beat a hasty retreat. If the mother dog is thin and blowing coat, that's normal and no cause for concern if she appears otherwise healthy and happy.

If you have wisely not limited your search to only local breeders, you'll want to be even more picky about the background of the litter *and* the breeder. Don't settle for just snapshots of nursing pups. If you're buying a show puppy, you are entitled to a video of the litter and detailed information on the parents.

Puppies exposed to young children have the benefit of better socialization. Akita breeders recognize how imperative socialization is and arrange for visitors. This is young David Dorsett working with a litter.

If you feel that this is pretentious and not really important, it may help you to know that dog shows evolved in order to determine which dogs were fit to reproduce. Whether it's a coonhound meet or a sheep herding contest, the purpose of all dog sports is to select the healthiest, hardiest, smartest, most beautiful breeding stock. It may surprise you to know that dog shows predate the Kentucky Derby as America's premier sporting event! So whether or not you plan to show your dog, demand proof

At eight weeks, Goldie shows off her exquisite head.

Amy is destined for the show ring. Practice setting up the show-bound puppy on the grooming table. Akita puppies from show breeders naturally take to standing in the proper stance.

that your puppy was created by conscientious people with top quality dogs that look and act like Akitas.

A pet puppy is ineligible to have any of its progeny registered. It is against the code of ethics of the national breed club, The Akita Club of America, to issue unrestricted registration papers for any puppy other than one priced and sold as show/breeding quality. Although pet puppies should be wonderful examples of the breed, in order to keep overall breed quality at the highest level, only those dogs that have been validated as superior specimens should reproduce. They are the Olympic stars, the Academy Award winners of the canine world. Those of you who are interested in exhibiting your Akita should take note. Gold medalists don't "just happen." It takes training, conditioning, a lot of perseverance, and a bit of luck.

One of the dog fancy's most popular personalities, James P. Taylor continues to walk the walk, setting up this young Akita pup.

A health record will come with your quality puppy, detailing worming (at least twice) and shot records. Any other trips to the vet should be documented. If the litter is treated for any illnesses, it doesn't mean the puppy has to be rejected but it's important information your vet should have.

When viewing a litter at eight weeks, consider the overall size, impressive bone, correct head shape and type, tiny ears and full coats. These puppies from O'BJ have more than their share in all categories.

HOUSEBREAKING Your Akita

A word of advice regarding use of the two most common commands "no" and "come here" is appropriate. Many owners find themselves absentmindedly saying "no" to a puppy that isn't really doing anything wrong. A puppy does not see into the future. He will be confused. Perhaps he was only thinking about coming over to give you a kiss—remember the little boy who cried wolf? Don't say "no" unless the puppy is actually misbehaving. Then use the command in a forceful, sharp, abrupt tone of voice and be prepared to enforce obedience. In other words, do not bother giving a command unless you are willing to take the time to enforce it. Likewise, do not constantly say "come here" when you really mean "no" or "stop that." Only call the puppy when you really want him to come to you and then reward him with a loving pat or a tidbit of food. In this way, a puppy never learns to disobey commands for he has never been allowed to disobey. If you begin conditioning him at this early age, he will remain obedient throughout his life.

Try not to confuse your Akita puppy. Say what you mean and say it in a word or two. Puppies are easily confused and most impressionable when very young.

Housebreaking your Akita should be a snap. If he wasn't shipped to you in a crate, then purchase one large enough to suit him as an adult. I recommend an open wire crate, especially for adult males who seem to resent being closed in where they cannot see and supervise the world around them!

For the first week or two, keep your puppy in the crate unless he's under the direct supervision of an adult family member. Feed him in the crate. He will come to regard this as his private den. Do not disturb or play with him when he's in his den. Like human children, he requires uninterrupted rest. When he awakens, immediately take him outside to relieve himself. Don't play with him or talk to him while he goes about that important business; just stand quietly. When he has begun to eliminate, praise him, using the same word or phrase each time like "good boy, go potty, go potty." He will soon associate those words and your praise with the elimination process and can therefore be prompted to hurry up when the weather is bad or when you have an important engagement. Take him out frequently, preferably a little further from the house each time, always using the stimulus word as he eliminates. When his tank is empty, take him back inside and allow him the freedom to explore the

Take the puppy out after each meal to do his business. This is not the time for play. Take him to the same place every time so that he knows what's expected.

65

Akitas are exceptionally clean and housebreak with ease. Paper training may be used as a transitional stage in housebreaking though many trainers advise against it.

house or to follow you from room to room.

The puppy should not be fed after 7 P.M., depending on what time you retire. Make sure there's plenty of time between his most recent fuel up and his last pit stop for the evening and he should sleep contentedly through the night.

If he cries, ignore it. Better to ignore him one night than to have him win the first round the first night. If his whimpering becomes a serious "help me" signal of distress, it may indicate a previously incomplete pit stop.

Get up quietly and with no ado take him to the "bathroom," ignoring his joy at your midnight response. He will quickly remember what he was crying about and you can both get back in bed. He'll whimper. Turn the radio on or put a pillow over your head.

Akitas are exceptionally clean house dogs so the housebreaking process, if followed consistently and with a mind to his natural functions, should be completed in a few days. Male puppies, like little boys, will urinate more frequently.

The first six months of ownership will lay the foundation for a lifetime of quality companionship. Don't begrudge the extra time. Bad day at work? A few quiet moments with the only friend who doesn't care what you did wrong, one who will listen attentively to your problems and agree with you without reservation.... well, it can make all the difference in how your evening goes.

Crates are the key to an unsoiled kingdom. Dogs learn not to mess in their sleeping area, hence they will not soil their crates. Don't expect too much too fast. A puppy simply cannot hold himself for hours on end.

You have an incredible opportunity to mold a friend who is socially acceptable, interesting, well mannered, of exceptional intellect, handsome (or beautiful, as the case may be), loyal, intuitive about your other friends, bi-lingual, and never asks to borrow money!

He will be the best friend you'll ever have.

STANDARD for the Akita

A breed standard is the criterion by which the appearance (and to a certain extent, the temperament as well) of any given dog is made subject to objective measurement. Basically, the standard for any breed is a definition of the perfect dog to which all specimens of the breed are compared. Breed standards are always subject to change through review by the national breed club for each dog, so it is always wise to keep up with developments in a breed by checking the publications of your national kennel club.

Ch. The Widow-Maker O'BJ is about as close to the "living standard" as an Akita can get. Winning one of his ten Bests in Show with breeder-handler B.J. Andrews.

The massive head, flat and broad skull, broad and full muzzle and powerful jaws define the correct type for the Akita head. This desirable head belongs to The Widow-Maker (photographed at ten years of age).

AMERICAN KENNEL CLUB STANDARD FOR THE AKITA

General Appearance—Large, powerful, alert, with much substance and heavy bone. The broad head, forming a blunt triangle, with deep muzzle, small eyes and erect ears carried forward in line with back of neck, is characteristic of the breed. The large, curled tail, balancing the broad head, is also characteristic of the breed.

Head—Massive but in balance with body; free of wrinkle when at ease. Skull flat between ears and broad; jaws square and powerful with minimal dewlap. Head forms a blunt triangle when viewed from above. *Fault*—Narrow or snipy head. *Muzzle*—Broad and full. Distance from nose to stop is to distance from stop to occiput as 2 is to 3. *Stop*—Well defined, but not too abrupt. A shallow furrow extends well up forehead. *Nose*—Broad and black. Liver permitted on white Akitas, but black always preferred. *Disqualifications*—Butterfly nose or total lack of pigmentation on nose. *Ears*—The ears of the Akita are characteristic of the breed. They are strongly erect and small in relation to rest of head. If ear is folded forward for measuring length, tip will touch upper eye rim. Ears are triangular, slightly rounded at tip, wide at base, set wide on head but not too low, and carried slightly forward over eyes in line with back of neck. *Disqualification*—Drop or broken ears. *Eyes*—Dark brown, small, deep-set and triangular in shape. Eye rims black and tight. *Lips and Tongue*—Lips black and not pendulous; tongue pink. *Teeth*—Strong with scissors bite preferred. but level bite acceptable. *Disqualification*—Noticeably undershot or overshot.

A bitch of bitches, this is the number-one Akita dam of all time, Ch. The Mad Hatter O'BJ, ROMXP. A specialty winner herself, Hatter has produced 16 champions and is the producer of some all time top winners in several countries.

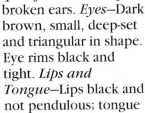

Neck and Body—*Neck*—Thick and muscular; comparatively short, widening gradually toward shoulders. A pronounced crest blends in with base of skull. *Body*—Longer than high, as 10 is to 9 in males; 11 to 9 in bitches. Chest wide and deep; depth of chest is one-half height of dog at shoulder. Ribs well sprung, brisket well developed. Level back with firmly-muscled loin and moderate tuck-up. Skin pliant but not loose. *Serious Faults*—Light bone, rangy body.

Tail—Large and full, set high and carried over back or against flank in a three-quarter, full, or double curl, always

Ch. O'BJ BigSon of Sachmo, ROMXP held several show ring records and is the third top sire of all time. He was a powerful, typey Akita male handled to many prestigious wins by the author.

dipping to or below level of back. On a three-quarter curl, tip drops well down flank. Root large and strong. Tail bone reaches hock when let down. Hair coarse, straight and full, with no appearance of a plume. *Disqualification*—Sickle or uncurled tail.

Forequarters and Hindquarters—*Forequarters*—Shoulders strong and powerful with moderate layback. Forelegs heavy-boned and straight as viewed from front. Angle of pastern 15 degrees forward from vertical. *Faults*—Elbows in or out, loose shoulders. *Hindquarters*—Width, muscular development and bone comparable to forequarters. Upper thighs well developed. Stifle moderately bent and hocks well

let down, turning neither in nor out. *Dewclaws*—On front legs generally not removed; dewclaws on hind legs generally removed. *Feet*—Cat feet, well knuckled up with thick pads. Feet straight ahead.

Coat—Double-coated. Undercoat thick, soft, dense and shorter than outer coat. Outer coat straight, harsh and standing somewhat off body. Hair on head, legs and ears short. Length of hair at withers and rump approximately two inches, which is slightly longer than on rest of body, except tail, where coat is longest and most profuse. *Fault*—Any indication of ruff or feathering.

The head of a bear! Ch. Classic's Sumo Mi Sun owned by Dave and Lee Ana Dorsett.

Color—Any color including white; brindle; or pinto. Colors are brilliant and clear and markings are well balanced, with or without mask or blaze. White Akitas have no mask. Pinto has a white background with large, evenly placed patches covering head and more than one-third of body. Undercoat may be a different color from outer coat.

Gait—Brisk and powerful with strides of moderate length. Back remains strong, firm and level. Rear legs move in line with front legs.

Size—Males 26 to 28 inches at the withers; bitches 24 to 26 inches. *Disqualification*—dogs under 25 inches; bitches under 23 inches.

Temperament—Alert and responsive, dignified and courageous. Aggressive toward other dogs.

Ch. The Joker's Wild O'BJ (son of The Widow-Maker out of The Mad Hatter) shown by former owner Roger Kaplan. Joker is exceptionally sound, solidly built, and is a best in show and #1 All-systems "Mismark."

DISQUALIFICATIONS
Butterfly nose or total lack of pigmentation on nose.

Drop or broken ears.

Noticeably undershot or overshot.

Sickle or uncurled tail.

Dogs under 25 inches; bitches under 23 inches.

SPORT of Purebred Dogs

Welcome to the exciting and sometimes frustrating sport of dogs. No doubt you are trying to learn more about dogs or you wouldn't be deep into this book. This section covers the basics that may entice you, further your knowledge and help you to understand the dog world. If you decide to give showing, obedience or any other dog activities a try, then I suggest you seek further help from the appropriate source.

Dog showing has been a very popular sport for a long time and has been taken quite seriously by some. Others only enjoy it as a hobby.

The Kennel Club in England was formed in 1859, the American Kennel Club was established in 1884 and the Canadian Kennel Club was formed in 1888. The purpose of these clubs was to register purebred dogs and maintain their Stud Books. In the beginning, the concept of registering dogs was not readily accepted. More than 36 million dogs have been enrolled in the AKC Stud Book since its inception in 1888. Presently the kennel clubs not

The dog sport requires commitment and know-how, two virtues known too well by this team: Ch. Cat in the Hat O'BJ and James P. Taylor. "Catter" is shown finishing her championship under James's expert handling.

only register dogs but adopt and enforce rules and regulations governing dog shows, obedience trials and field trials. Over the years they have fostered and encouraged interest in the health and welfare of the purebred dog. They routinely donate funds to veterinary research for study on genetic disorders.

Below are the addresses of the kennel clubs in the United States, Great Britain and Canada.

The American Kennel Club
51 Madison Avenue
New York, NY 10010
(Their registry is located at:
5580Centerview Dr., STE 200,
Raleigh, NC 27606-3390)

The Kennel Club
1 Clarges Street
Piccadilly, London, WIY 8AB,
England

The Canadian Kennel Club
111 Eglinton Avenue
East Toronto, Ontario M6S 4V7
Canada

Overhill's Midnight Runner as a puppy racing her way to the top in English competition. Breeder-owner-handled by Meg Purnell-Carpeneter.

Today there are numerous activities that are enjoyable for both the dog and the handler. Some of the activities include conformation showing, obedience competition, tracking, agility, the Canine Good Citizen Certificate, and a wide range of instinct tests that vary from breed to breed. Where you start depends upon your goals which early on may not be readily apparent.

PUPPY KINDERGARTEN
Every puppy will benefit from this class. PKT is the foundation for all future dog activities from conformation to "couch potatoes." Pet owners should make an effort to attend even if they never expect to show their dog. The

Praise the Akita puppy for proper behavior. Encouraging a puppy to want to do well makes later training easier and faster.

class is designed for puppies about three months of age with graduation at approximately five months of age. All the puppies will be in the same age group and, even though some may be a little unruly, there should not be any real problem. This class will teach the puppy some beginning obedience. As in all obedience classes the owner learns how to train his own dog. The PKT class gives the puppy the opportunity to interact with other puppies in the same age group and exposes him to strangers, which is very important. Some dogs grow up with behavior problems, one of them being fear of strangers. As you can see, there can be much to gain from this class.

There are some basic obedience exercises that every dog should learn. Some of these can be started with puppy kindergarten.

Sit

One way of teaching the sit is to have your dog on your left side with the leash in your right hand, close to the collar. Pull up on the leash and at the same time reach around his hindlegs with your left hand and tuck them in. As you are doing this say, "Beau, sit." Always use the dog's name when you give an active command. Some owners like to use a treat holding it over the dog's head. The dog will need to sit to get the treat. Encourage the dog to hold the sit for a few seconds, which will eventually be the beginning of the Sit/Stay. Depending on how cooperative he is, you can rub him under the chin or stroke his back. It is a good time to establish eye contact.

Akita puppies do well in handling classes or basic obedience classes. The more people your Akita meets as a puppy, the more manageable and personable he will be as an adult.

Down

Sit the dog on your left side and kneel down beside him with the leash in your right hand. Reach over him with your left hand and grasp his left foreleg. With your right hand, take his right foreleg and pull his legs forward while you say, "Beau, down." If he tries to get up, lean on his shoulder to encourage him to stay down. It will relax your dog if you stroke his back while he is down. Try to encourage him to stay down for a few seconds as preparation for the Down/Stay.

Heel

The definition of heeling is the dog walking under control at your left heel. Your puppy will learn controlled walking in the puppy kindergarten class, which will eventually lead to heeling. The command is "Beau, heel," and you start off briskly with your left foot. Your leash is in your right hand and your left hand is holding it about half way down. Your left hand should be able to control the leash and there should be a little slack in it. You want him to walk with you with your leg somewhere between his nose and his shoulder. You need to encourage him to stay with you, not forging (in front of you) or lagging behind you. It is best to keep him on a fairly short lead. Do not allow the lead to become tight. It is far better to give him a little jerk when necessary and remind him to heel. When you come to a halt, be prepared physically to make him sit. It takes practice to become coordinated. There are excellent books on training that you may wish to purchase. Your instructor should be able to recommend one for you.

When the puppy is in the Down position, praise him gently and assure him that all is well.

Recall

This quite possibly is the most important exercise you will ever teach. It should be a pleasant experience. The puppy may learn to do random recalls while being attached to a long line such as a clothes line. Later the exercise will start with the dog sitting and staying until called. The command is "Beau, come." Let your command be happy. You want your dog to come willingly and

Puppies trained for the show ring may not be taught the Sit command right away. It's more important that the puppy learns to Stand and Stay.

faithfully. The recall could save his life if he sneaks out the door. In practicing the recall, let him jump on you or touch you before you reach for him. If he is shy, then kneel down to

This puppy is too low on the leg to compete in the show ring. Akitas should never appear "dumpy" at any age.

his level. Reaching for the insecure dog could frighten him, and he may not be willing to come again in the future. Lots of praise and a treat would be in

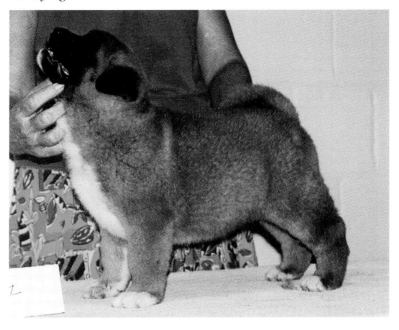

order whenever you do a recall. Under no circumstances should you ever correct your dog when he has come to you. Later in formal obedience your dog will be required to sit in front of you after recalling and then go to heel position.

CONFORMATION

Conformation showing is our oldest dog show sport. This type of showing is based on the dog's appearance—that is his structure, movement and attitude. When considering this type of showing, you need to be aware of your breed's standard and be able to evaluate your dog compared to that standard. The breeder of your puppy or other experienced breeders would be good sources for such an evaluation. Puppies can go through lots of changes over a period of time. I always say most puppies start out as promising hopefuls and then after maturing may be disappointing as show candidates. Even so this should not deter them from being excellent pets.

Although the author has bred more Akita champions than any other breeder, she is also revered for handling most of her dogs to their titles. With Ch. The Widow-Maker O'BJ at the end of the author's lead, the team became the number-one owner-handled Akita in the history of the breed.

Usually conformation training classes are offered by the local kennel or obedience clubs. These are excellent places for training puppies. The puppy should be able to walk on a lead before entering such a class. Proper ring procedure and technique for posing (stacking) the dog will be demonstrated as well as gaiting the dog. Usually certain patterns are used in the

A young red male Akita showing good color and excellent structure. Only if your Akita will be competitive in the show ring should you consider investing time and money into the sport. It pays to buy the best puppy you can afford if you intend to show.

ring such as the triangle or the "L." Conformation class, like the PKT class, will give your youngster the opportunity to socialize with different breeds of dogs and humans too. It takes some time to learn the routine of conformation showing. Usually one starts at the puppy matches which may be AKC Sanctioned or Fun Matches. These matches are generally for puppies from two or three months to a year old, and there may be classes for the adult over the age of 12 months. Similar to point shows, the classes are divided by sex and after completion of the classes in that breed or variety, the class winners compete for Best of Breed or Variety. The winner goes on to compete in the Group and the Group winners compete for Best in Match. No championship points are awarded for match wins.

A few matches can be great training for puppies even though there is no intention to go on showing. Matches enable the puppy to meet new people and be handled by a stranger—the judge. It is also a change of environment, which broadens the horizon for both dog and handler. Matches and other dog activities boost the confidence of the handler and especially the younger handlers.

Earning an AKC championship is built on a point system, which is different from Great Britain. To become an AKC Champion of Record the dog must earn 15 points. The number of points earned each time depends upon the number of dogs in competition. The number of points available at each show depends upon the breed, its sex and the location of the show. The United States is divided into ten AKC zones. Each zone has its own set of points. The purpose of the zones is to try to equalize the points available from breed to breed and area to area.The AKC adjusts the point scale annually.

The number of points that can be won at a show are between one and five. Three-, four- and five-point wins are considered majors. Not only does the dog need 15 points won under three different judges, but those points must include two majors under two different judges. Canada also works on a point system but majors are not required.

Dogs always show before bitches. The classes available to those seeking points are: Puppy (which may be divided into 6 to 9 months and 9 to 12 months); 12 to 18 months; Novice; Bred-by-Exhibitor; American-bred; and Open. The class winners of the same sex of each breed or variety compete against each other for Winners Dog and Winners Bitch. A Reserve Winners Dog and Reserve Winners Bitch are also awarded but do not carry any points unless the Winners win is disallowed by AKC. The Winners Dog and Bitch compete with the specials (those dogs that have attained championship) for Best of Breed or Variety, Best of Winners and Best of Opposite Sex. It is possible to pick up an extra point or even a major if the points are higher for the defeated winner than those of Best of Winners. The latter would get the higher total from the defeated winner.

Attention all judges: This is a bear dog not a bird dog. Both dogs and bitches must have substance to be called Akita. Puppy bitch O'BJ Canduit Tuya taking Best of Opposite from the classes.

At an all-breed show, each Best of Breed or Variety winner will go on to his respective Group and then the Group winners will compete against each other for Best in Show. There are seven Groups: Sporting, Hounds,

Working, Terriers, Toys, Non-Sporting and Herding. Obviously there are no Groups at speciality shows (those shows that have only one breed or a show such as the American Spaniel Club's Flushing Spaniel Show, which is for all flushing spaniel breeds).

Earning a championship in England is somewhat different since they do not have a point system. Challenge Certificates are awarded if the judge feels the dog is deserving regardless of the number of dogs in competition. A dog must earn three Challenge Certificates under three different judges, with at least one of these Certificates being won after the age of 12 months. Competition is very strong and entries may be higher than they are in the U.S. The Kennel Club's Challenge Certificates are only available at Championship Shows.

In England, The Kennel Club regulations require that certain dogs, Border Collies and Gundog breeds, qualify in a working capacity (i.e., obedience or field trials) before becoming a full Champion. If they do not qualify in the working aspect, then they are designated a Show Champion, which is equivalent to the AKC's Champion of Record. A Gundog may be granted the title of Field Trial Champion (FT Ch.) if it passes all the tests in the field but would also have to qualify in conformation before becoming a full Champion. A Border Collie that earns the title of Obedience Champion (Ob Ch.) must also qualify in the conformation ring before becoming a Champion.

The U.S. doesn't have a designation full Champion but does award for Dual and Triple Champions. The Dual Champion must be a Champion of Record, and either Champion Tracker, Herding Champion, Obedience Trial Champion or Field Champion. Any dog that has been awarded the titles of

Champion of Record, and any two of the following: Champion Tracker, Herding Champion, Obedience Trial Champion or Field Champion, may be designated as a Triple Champion.

Ch. Mokusei's Zeus of Daitan-Ni at 16 months of age became a top winner and producer for owner Jeanne Galindo Hayes.

This is "Dude" (Ch. Chiheisen's Take It to the Maxx). Handled by Bruce Schultz, Dude won many groups and bests in show. Owned by S and F. Thomas, J. Machline and M. and C. Schipper.

The shows in England seem to put more emphasis on breeder judges than those in the U.S. There is much competition within the breeds. Therefore the quality of the individual breeds should be very good. In the United States we tend to have more "all around judges" (those that judge multiple breeds) and use the breeder judges at the specialty shows. Breeder judges are more familiar with their own breed since they are actively breeding that breed or did so at one time. Americans emphasize Group and Best in Show wins and promote them accordingly.

It is my understanding that the shows in England can be very large and extend over several days, with the Groups being scheduled on different days. I believe there is only one all-breed show in the U.S. that extends over two days, the

Westminster Kennel Club Show. In our country we have cluster shows, where several different clubs will use the same show site over consecutive days.

Westminster Kennel Club is our most prestigious show although the entry is limited to 2500. In recent years, entry has been limited to Champions. This show is more formal than the majority of the shows with the judges wearing formal attire and the handlers fashionably dressed. In most instances the quality of the dogs is superb. After all, it is a show of Champions. It is a good show to study the AKC registered breeds and is by far the most exciting—especially since it is televised! WKC is one of the few shows in this country that is still benched. This means the dog must be in his benched area during the show hours except when he is being groomed, in the ring, or being exercised.

Typically, the handlers are very particular about their appearances. They are careful not to wear something that will detract from their dog but will perhaps enhance it. American ring procedure is quite formal compared to that of other countries. I remember being reprimanded by a judge because I made a suggestion to a friend holding my second dog outside the ring. I certainly could have used more discretion so I would not call attention to myself. There is a certain etiquette expected between the judge and exhibitor and among the other exhibitors. Of course it is not always the case but the judge is supposed to be polite, not engaging in small talk or even acknowledging that he knows the handler. I understand that there is a more informal and

Ch. The Copy Cat O'BJ has won the Breed and Group over top males, not an easy feat for a female Akita. Owner, Lori Nichols.

relaxed atmosphere at the shows in other countries. For instance, the dress code is more casual. I can see where this might be more fun for the exhibitor and especially for the novice. This country is very handler-oriented in many of the breeds. It is true, in most instances, that the experienced professional handler can present the dog better and will have a feel for what a judge likes.

Ch. The Dame's On Target, ROMXP is the number four dam of all time, a litter sister to Widow-Maker, and the producer of top ranked and Best in Show progeny. Bred and owned by BJ and Bill Andrews.

In England, Crufts is The Kennel Club's own show and is most assuredly the largest dog show in the world. They've been known to have an entry of nearly 20,000, and the show lasts four days. Entry is only gained by qualifying through winning in specified classes at another Championship Show. Westminster is strictly conformation, but Crufts exhibitors and spectators enjoy not only conformation but obedience, agility and a multitude of exhibitions as well. Obedience was admitted in 1957 and agility in 1983.

If you are handling your own dog, please give some consideration to your apparel. For sure the dress code at matches is more informal than the point shows. However, you should wear something a little more appropriate than beach attire or ragged jeans and bare feet. If you check out the handlers and see what is presently fashionable, you'll catch on. Men usually dress with a shirt and tie and a nice sports coat. Whether you are male or female, you will want to wear comfortable clothes and shoes. You need to be able to run with your dog and you certainly don't want to take a chance of falling and hurting yourself. Heaven forbid, if nothing else, you'll upset your dog. Women usually wear a dress or two-piece outfit, preferably with pockets to carry bait, comb, brush, etc. In this case men are the lucky ones with all their pockets. Ladies, think about where your dress will be if you need to kneel on the floor and also think about running. Does it allow freedom to do so?

Years ago, after toting around all the baby paraphernalia, I found toting the dog and necessities a breeze. You need to take along dog; crate; ex pen (if you use one); extra newspaper; water pail and water; all required grooming equipment, including hair dryer and extension cord; table; chair for you; bait for dog and lunch for you and friends; and, last but not least, clean up materials, such as plastic bags, paper towels, and perhaps a bath towel and some shampoo—just in case. Don't forget your entry confirmation and directions to the show.

If you are showing in obedience, then you will want to wear pants. Many of our top obedience handlers wear pants that are color-coordinated with their dogs. The philosophy is that imperfections in the black dog will be less obvious next to your black pants.

Whether you are showing in conformation, Junior Showmanship or obedience, you need to watch the clock and be sure you are not late. It is customary to pick up your conformation armband a few minutes before the start of the class. They will not wait for you and if you are on the show grounds and not in the ring, you will upset everyone. It's a little more complicated picking up your obedience armband if you show later in the class. If you have not picked up your armband and they get to your number,

Checan's Ko Guma retrieving dumbbell for obedience trainer John Seaborn. This 21-month Akita student proves that Akitas can be trained with patience and know-how.

you may not be allowed to show. It's best to pick up your armband early, but then you may show earlier than expected if other handlers don't pick up. Customarily all conflicts should be discussed with the judge prior to the start of the class.

Junior Showmanship

The Junior Showmanship Class is a wonderful way to build self confidence even if there are no aspirations of staying with the dog-show game later in life. Frequently, Junior Showmanship becomes the background of those who become successful exhibitors/handlers in the future. In some instances it is taken very seriously, and success is measured in terms of wins. The Junior Handler is judged solely on his ability and skill in presenting his dog. The dog's conformation is not to be considered by the judge. Even so the condition and grooming of the dog may be a reflection upon the handler.

Usually the matches and point shows include different classes. The Junior Handler's dog may be entered in a breed or obedience class and even shown by another person in that class. Junior Showmanship classes are usually divided by age and perhaps sex. The age is determined by the handler's age on the day of the show. The classes are:

Novice Junior for those at least ten and under 14 years of age who at time of entry closing have not won three first places in a Novice Class at a licensed or member show.

Novice Senior for those at least 14 and under 18 years of age who at the time of entry closing have not won three first places in a Novice Class at a licensed or member show.

Open Junior for those at least ten and under 14 years of age who at the time of entry closing have won at least three first places in a Novice Junior Showmanship Class at a licensed or member show with competition present.

Open Senior for those at least 14 and under 18 years of age who at time of entry closing have won at least three first places in a Novice Junior Showmanship Class at a licensed or member show with competition present.

Junior Handlers must include their AKC Junior Handler number on each show entry. This needs to be obtained from the AKC.

Kota participating in a bench show sharing time and popcorn with a young friend. Owners, Phil and Wendy Reed.

CANINE GOOD CITIZEN

The AKC sponsors a program to encourage dog owners to train their dogs. Local clubs perform the pass/fail tests, and dogs who pass are awarded a Canine Good Citizen Certificate. Proof of vaccination is required at the time of participation. The test includes:

1. Accepting a friendly stranger.
2. Sitting politely for petting.
3. Appearance and grooming.

4. Walking on a loose leash.
5. Walking through a crowd.
6. Sit and down on command/staying in place.
7. Come when called.
8. Reaction to another dog.
9. Reactions to distractions.
10. Supervised separation.

If every Akita owner would subscribe to participating in community programs with their dogs, the breed would have better temperaments and better reputations.

If more effort was made by pet owners to accomplish these exercises, fewer dogs would be cast off to the humane shelter.

OBEDIENCE

Obedience is necessary, without a doubt, but it can also become a wonderful hobby or even an obsession. In my opinion, obedience classes and competition can provide wonderful companionship, not only with your dog but with your classmates or fellow competitors. It is always gratifying to discuss your dog's problems with others who have had similar experiences. The AKC acknowledged Obedience around 1936, and it has changed tremendously even though many of the exercises are basically the same. Today, obedience competition is just that—very competitive. Even so, it is possible for every obedience exhibitor to come home a winner (by earning qualifying scores) even though he/she may not earn a placement in the class.

Most of the obedience titles are awarded after earning three qualifying scores (legs) in the appropriate class under three different judges. These classes offer a perfect score of 200, which is extremely rare. Each of the class exercises has its own point value. A leg is earned after receiving a score of at least 170 and at least 50 percent of the points available in each exercise. The titles are:

Companion Dog–CD
This is called the Novice Class and the exercises are:

1. Heel on leash and figure 8	40 points
2. Stand for examination	30 points
3. Heel free	40 points
4. Recall	30 points
5. Long sit–one minute	30 points
6. Long down–three minutes	30 points
Maximum total score	200 points

Companion Dog Excellent–CDX
This is the Open Class and the exercises are:

1. Heel off leash and figure 8	40 points
2. Drop on recall	30 points
3. Retrieve on flat	20 points
4. Retrieve over high jump	30 points
5. Broad jump	20 points
6. Long sit–three minutes (out of sight)	30 points
7. Long down–five minutes (out of sight)	30 points
Maximum total score	200 points

Dog shows can be great fun when you and your dog become involved together. Here the author handles BigSon while being examined in the Working Group.

Utility Dog–UD

The Utility Class exercises are:

1.Signal Exercise	40 points
2.Scent discrimination-Article 1	30points
3.Scent discrimination-Article 2	30 points
4.Directed retrieve	30 points
5.Moving stand and examination	30 points
6.Directed jumping	40 points
Maximum total score	200 points

O'BJ royalty in Chile...this is "Queen" showing off a noble gait. Owned by Akitas Ace.

After achieving the UD title, you may feel inclined to go after the UDX and/or OTCh. The UDX (Utility Dog Excellent) title went into effect in January 1994. It is not easily attained. The title requires qualifying simultaneously ten times in Open B and Utility B but not necessarily at consecutive shows.

Although not sponsored by national kennel clubs, weight pull competitions have attracted Akitas and other Working breeds. These contests challenge a dog's concentration, strength and endurance.

The OT Ch(Obedience Trial Champion) is awarded after the dog has earned his UD and then goes on to earn 100 championship points, a first place in Utility, a first place in Open and another first place in either class. The

placements must be won under three different judges at all-breed obedience trials. The points are determined by the number of dogs competing in the Open B and Utility B classes. The OTCh title precedes the dog's name.

Obedience matches (AKC Sanctioned, Fun, and Show and Go) are usually available. Usually they are sponsored by the local obedience clubs. When preparing an obedience dog for a title, you will find matches very helpful. Fun Matches and Show and Go Matches are more lenient in allowing you to make corrections in the ring. I frequently train (correct) in the ring and inform the judge that I would like to do so and to please mark me "exhibition." This means that I will not be eligible for any prize. This type of training is usually very necessary for the Open and Utility Classes. AKC Sanctioned Obedience Matches do not allow corrections in the ring since they must abide by the AKC Obedience Regulations. If you are interested in showing in obedience, then you should contact the AKC for a copy of the Obedience Regulations.

TRACKING

Tracking is officially classified obedience, but I feel it should have its own category. There are three tracking titles available: Tracking Dog (TD), Tracking Dog Excellent (TDX), Variable Surface Tracking (VST). If all three tracking titles are obtained, then the dog officially becomes a CT (Champion Tracker). The CT will go in front of the dog's name.

A TD may be earned anytime and does not have to follow the other obedience titles. There are many exhibitors that prefer tracking to obedience, and there are others like myself

Ch. Willodeen O'PR Kyojin Kamiaki in motion. Owners, David and Gloria Ketcher.

Kiskas Jezabel's claim to fame is that she won the first bitch Challenge Certificate for an Akita in England.

that do both. In my experience with small dogs, I prefer to earn the CD and CDX before attempting tracking. My reasoning is that small dogs are closer to the mat in the obedience rings and therefore it's too easy to put the nose down and sniff. Tracking encourages sniffing. Of course this depends on the dog. I've had some dogs that tracked around the ring and others (TDXs) who wouldn't think of sniffing in the ring.

Tracking Dog–TD

A dog must be certified by an AKC tracking judge that he is ready to perform in an AKC test. The AKC can provide the names of tracking judges in your area that you can contact for certification. Depending on where you live, you may have to travel a distance if there is no local tracking judge. The certification track will be equivalent to a regular AKC track. A regulation track must be 440 to 500 yards long with at least two right-angle turns out in the open. The track will be aged 30 minutes to two hours. The handler has two starting flags at the beginning of the track to indicate the direction started. The dog works on a harness and 40-foot lead and must work at least 20 feet in front of the handler. An article (either a dark glove or

wallet) will be dropped at the end of the track, and the dog must indicate it but not necessarily retrieve it.

People always ask me what the dog tracks. In my opinion, initially, the beginner on the short-aged track tracks the tracklayer. Eventually the dog learns to track the disturbed vegetation and learns to differentiate between tracks. Getting started with tracking requires reading the AKC regulations and a good book on tracking plus finding other tracking enthusiasts. I like to work on the buddy system. That is—we lay tracks for each other so we can practice blind tracks. It is possible to train on your own, but if you are a beginner, it is a lot more entertaining to track with a buddy. Tracking is my favorite dog sport. It's rewarding seeing the dog use his natural ability.

Tracking Dog Excellent—TDX

The TDX track is 800 to 1000 yards long and is aged three to five hours. There will be five to seven turns. An article is left at the starting flag, and three other articles must be indicated on the track. There is only one flag at the start, so it is a blind start. Approximately one and a half hours after the track is laid, two tracklayers will cross over the track at two different places to test the dog's ability to stay with the original track. There will be at least two obstacles on the track such as a change of cover, fences, creeks, ditches, etc. The dog must have a TD before entering a TDX. There is no certification required for a TDX.

Variable Surface Tracking—VST

This test came into effect September 1995. The dog must have a TD earned at least six months prior to entering this test. The track is 600 to 800 yards long and shall have a minimum of three different surfaces. Vegetation shall be included along with two areas devoid of vegetation

Who can doubt the Akita's trainability when viewing Akita Kuro Inu of Oozora, CDX practicing the high jump? Companion Dog Excellent is one of the highest titles an obedience dog can attain.

such as concrete, asphalt, gravel, sand, hard pan or mulch. The areas devoid of vegetation shall comprise at least one-third to one-half of the track. The track is aged three to five hours. There will be four to eight turns and four numbered articles including one leather, one plastic, one metal and one fabric dropped on the track. There is one starting flag. The handler will work at least 10 feet from the dog.

AGILITY

Agility was first introduced by John Varley in England at the Crufts Dog Show, February 1978, but Peter Meanwell, competitor and judge, actually developed the idea. It was officially recognized in the early '80s. Agility is extremely popular in England and Canada and growing in popularity in the U.S. The AKC acknowledged agility in August 1994. Dogs must be at least 12 months of age to be entered. It is a fascinating sport that the dog, handler and spectators enjoy to the utmost. Agility is a spectator sport! The dog performs off lead. The handler either runs with his dog or positions himself

Ch. The Mad Hatter O'BJ earned her claim to fame in the whelping box and became the number one dam of all time. She was owned and bred by B.J. and Bill Andrews.

With training and proper handling, Akitas can excel in obedience trials. This Akita is demonstrating free heeling in Novice Obedience.

on the course and directs his dog with verbal and hand signals over a timed course over or through a variety of obstacles including a time out or pause. One of the main drawbacks to agility is finding a place to train. The obstacles take up a lot of space and it is very time consuming to put up and take down courses.

The titles earned at AKC agility trials are Novice Agility Dog (NAD), Open Agility Dog (OAD), Agility Dog Excellent (ADX), and Master Agility Excellent (MAX). In order to acquire an agility title, a dog must earn a qualifying score in its respective class on three separate occasions under two different judges. The MAX will be awarded after earning ten qualifying scores in the Agility Excellent Class.

HEALTH CARE For Your Akita

Veterinary medicine has become far more sophisticated than what was available to our ancestors. This can be attributed to the increase in household pets and consequently the demand for better care for them. Also human medicine has become far more complex. Today diagnostic testing in veterinary medicine parallels human diagnostics. Because of better technology we can expect our pets to live healthier lives thereby increasing their life spans.

THE FIRST CHECK UP

You will want to take your new puppy/dog in for its first check up within 48 to 72 hours after acquiring it. Many breeders strongly recommend this check up and so do the humane shelters. A puppy/dog can appear healthy but it may have a serious problem that is not apparent to the layman. Most pets have some type of a minor flaw that may never cause a real problem.

At nine weeks this longcoat Akita is the picture of good health and vitality. Your veterinarian should give your new Akita puppy a complete physical to ensure that the health of the puppy has not been misrepresented.

Unfortunately if he/she should have a serious problem, you will want to consider the consequences of keeping the pet and the attachments that will be formed, which may be broken prematurely. Keep in mind there are many healthy dogs looking for good homes.

This first check up is a good time to establish yourself with the veterinarian and learn the office policy regarding their hours and how they handle emergencies. Usually the breeder or another conscientious pet owner is a good reference for locating a capable veterinarian. You should be aware that not all veterinarians give the same quality of service. Please do not make your selection on the least expensive clinic, as they may be short changing your pet. There is the possibility that eventually it will cost you more due to improper diagnosis,

treatment, etc. If you are selecting a new veterinarian, feel free to ask for a tour of the clinic. You should inquire about making an appointment for a tour since all clinics are working clinics, and therefore may not be available all day for sightseers. You may worry less if you see where your pet will be spending the day if he ever needs to be hospitalized.

THE PHYSICAL EXAM

Your veterinarian will check your pet's overall condition, which includes listening to the heart; checking the respiration; feeling the abdomen, muscles and joints; checking the mouth, which includes the gum color and signs of gum disease along with plaque buildup; checking the ears for signs of an infection or ear mites; examining the eyes; and, last but not least, checking the condition of the skin and coat.

He should ask you questions regarding your pet's eating and elimination habits and invite you to relay your questions. It is a good idea to prepare a list so as not to forget anything. He should discuss the proper diet and the quantity to be fed. If this should differ from your breeder's recommendation, then you should convey to him the breeder's choice and see if he approves. If he recommends changing the diet, then this should be done over a few days so as not to cause a gastrointestinal upset. It is customary to take in a fresh stool sample (just a small amount) for a test for intestinal parasites. It must be fresh, preferably within 12 hours, since the eggs hatch quickly and after hatching will not be observed under the microscope. If your pet isn't obliging then, usually the technician can take one in the clinic.

IMMUNIZATIONS

It is important that you take your puppy/dog's vaccination record with you on your first visit. In case of a puppy, presumably the breeder has seen to the vaccinations up to the time you acquired custody. Veterinarians differ in their vaccination protocol. It is not unusual for your puppy to have received vaccinations for distemper, hepatitis, leptospirosis, parvovirus and parainfluenza every two to three weeks from the age of seven weeks. Usually this is a combined injection and is typically called the DHLPP. The DHLPP is given through at least 12 to 14 weeks of age, and it is customary to continue with another parvovirus vaccine at 16 to 18 weeks. You may wonder why so many immunizations are necessary. No one knows for sure when the puppy's maternal antibodies are gone, although it is customarily accepted that distemper antibodies are gone by 12 weeks. Usually parvovirus antibodies are gone by 16 to 18 weeks of age. However, it is possible for the maternal antibodies to be gone at a much earlier age or even a later age. Therefore immunizations are started at an early age. The vaccine will not give immunity as long as there are maternal antibodies.

Before puppies are released to homes, they typically have received one or two immunizations. Your veterinarian will put your Akita puppy on a vaccination schedule at the first visit.

The rabies vaccination is given at three or six months of age depending on your local laws. A vaccine for bordetella (kennel cough)can be given anytime from the age of seven weeks. The coronavirus is not commonly given unless there is a problem locally. The Lyme vaccine is often recommended in endemic areas. Lyme disease has been reported in 47 states.

Distemper

This is virtually an incurable disease. If the dog recovers, he is subject to severe nervous disorders. The virus attacks every tissue in the body and resembles a bad cold with a fever. It can cause a runny nose and eyes and cause gastrointestinal disorders, including a poor appetite, vomiting and diarrhea. The virus is carried by raccoons, foxes, wolves, mink and other dogs. Unvaccinated youngsters and senior citizens are very susceptible. This is still a common disease.

Hepatitis

This is a virus that is most serious in very young dogs. It is spread by contact with an infected animal or its stool or urine. The virus affects the liver and kidneys and is characterized by high fever, depression and lack of appetite. Recovered animals may be afflicted with chronic illnesses.

Leptospirosis

This is a bacterial disease transmitted by contact with the urine of an infected dog, rat or other wildlife. It produces severe symptoms of fever, depression, jaundice and internal bleeding and was fatal before the vaccine was developed. Recovered dogs can be carriers, and the disease can be transmitted from dogs to humans.

Parvovirus

This was first noted in the late 1970s and is still a fatal disease. However, with proper vaccinations, early diagnosis and prompt treatment, it is a manageable disease. It attacks the bone marrow and intestinal tract. The symptoms include depression, loss of appetite, vomiting, diarrhea and collapse. Immediate medical attention is of the essence.

Rabies

This is shed in the saliva and is carried by raccoons, skunks, foxes, other dogs and cats. It attacks nerve tissue, resulting in paralysis and death. Rabies can be transmitted to people and is virtually always fatal. This disease is reappearing in the suburbs.

Bordetella (Kennel Cough)

The symptoms are coughing, sneezing, hacking and retching accompanied by nasal discharge usually lasting from a few days

Kennel cough is a highly contagious disease. Boarding kennels require that dogs are vaccinated a few weeks prior to their visit.

to several weeks. There are several disease-producing organisms responsible for this disease. The present vaccines are helpful but do not protect for all the strains. It usually is not life threatening but in some instances it can progress to a serious bronchopneumonia. The disease is highly contagious. The vaccination should be given routinely for dogs that come in contact with other dogs, such as through boarding, training class or visits to the groomer.

Bordetella attached to canine cilia. This disease is not life-threatening but can progress to a serious bronchopneumonia.

Coronavirus

This is usually self limiting and not life threatening. It was first noted in the late '70s about a year before parvovirus. The virus produces a yellow/brown stool and there may be depression, vomiting and diarrhea.

Even the most healthy puppies can have worms and other microbes, thus all breeders subscribe to vaccinating and worming puppies. These wormless future champions belong to Tim and Cindy Burns.

Lyme Disease

This was first diagnosed in

the United States in 1976 in Lyme, CT in people who lived in close proximity to the deer tick. Symptoms may include acute lameness, fever, swelling of joints and loss of appetite. Your veterinarian can advise you if you live in an endemic area.

After your puppy has completed his puppy vaccinations, you will continue to booster the DHLPP once a year. It is customary to booster the rabies one year after the first vaccine and then, depending on where you live, it should be boostered every year or every three years. This depends on your local laws.

ANNUAL VISIT

I would like to impress the importance of the annual check up, which would include the booster vaccinations, check for intestinal parasites and test for heartworm. Today in our very busy world it is rush, rush and see "how much you can get for how little." Unbelievably, some non-veterinary businesses have entered into the vaccination business. More harm than good can come to your dog through improper vaccinations, possibly from inferior vaccines and/or the wrong schedule. More than likely you truly care about your companion dog and over the years you have devoted much time and expense to his well being. Perhaps you are unaware that a vaccination is not just a vaccination. There is more involved. Please, please follow through with regular physical examinations. It is so important for your veterinarian to know your dog and this is especially true during middle age through the geriatric years. More than likely your older dog will require more than one physical a year. The annual physical is good preventive medicine. Through early diagnosis and subsequent treatment your dog can maintain a longer and better quality of life.

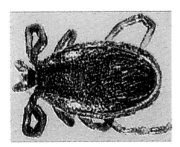

Ticks have forever been a common parasite of both man and dog. Courtesy of Virbac Laboratories, Inc., Fort Worth, Texas.

Once properly vaccinated, the nine week old needs socialization with lots of people and different places. Don't isolate your Akita puppy. This is Topper with exchange student Keiichi.

Intestinal Parasites

Hookworms

These are almost microscopic intestinal worms that can cause anemia and therefore serious problems, including death, in young puppies. Hookworms can be transmitted to humans through penetration of the skin. Puppies may be born with them.

Roundworms

These are spaghetti-like worms that can cause a potbellied appearance and dull coat along with more severe symptoms, such as vomiting, diarrhea and coughing. Puppies acquire these while in the mother's uterus and through lactation. Both hookworms and roundworms may be acquired through ingestion.

As much good-smelling fun as dogs have in grass, your Akita can pick up ticks, fleas, or other undesirables—not to mention suffer from a grass allergy or other irritation.

Whipworms

These have a three-month life cycle and are not acquired through the dam. They cause intermittent diarrhea usually with mucus. Whipworms are possibly the most difficult worm to eradicate. Their eggs are very resistant to most environmental factors and can last for years until the proper conditions enable them to mature. Whipworms are seldom seen in the stool.

Intestinal parasites are more prevalent in some areas than others. Climate, soil and contamination are big factors contributing to the incidence of intestinal parasites. Eggs are passed in the stool, lay on the ground and then become infective in a certain number of days. Each of the above worms has a different life cycle. Your best chance of becoming and remaining worm-free is to always pooper-scoop your yard. A fenced-in yard keeps stray dogs out, which is certainly helpful.

I would recommend having a fecal examination on your dog twice a year or more often if there is a problem. If your dog has a positive fecal sample, then he will be given the appropriate medication and you will be asked to bring back another stool sample in a certain period of time (depending on the type of worm) and then be rewormed. This process goes on until he has at least two negative samples. The different types of worms require different medications. You will be wasting your money and doing your dog an injustice by buying over-the-counter medication without first consulting your veterinarian.

Whipworms are hard to find unless one strains the feces, and this is best left to a veterinarian. These are adult whipworms.

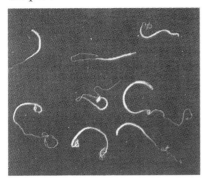

OTHER INTERNAL PARASITES

Coccidiosis and Giardiasis

These protozoal infections usually affect puppies, especially in places where large numbers of puppies are brought together. Older dogs may harbor these infections but do not show signs unless they are stressed. Symptoms include diarrhea, weight loss and lack of appetite. These infections are not always apparent in the fecal examination.

Tapeworms

Seldom apparent on fecal floatation, they are diagnosed frequently as rice-like segments around the dog's anus and the base of the tail. Tapeworms are long, flat and ribbon like, sometimes several feet in length, and made up of many segments about five-eighths of an inch long. The two most common types of tapeworms found

in the dog are:
(1) First the larval form of the flea tapeworm parasite must mature in an intermediate host, the flea, before it can become infective. Your dog acquires this by ingesting the flea through licking and chewing.
(2) Rabbits, rodents and certain large game animals serve as intermediate hosts for other species of tapeworms. If your dog should eat one of these infected hosts, then he can acquire tapeworms.

HEARTWORM DISEASE

This is a worm that resides in the heart and adjacent blood vessels of the lung that produces microfilaria, which circulate in the bloodstream. It is possible for a dog to be infected with any number of worms from one to a hundred that can be 6 to 14 inches long. It is a life-threatening disease, expensive to treat and easily prevented. Depending on where you live, your veterinarian may recommend a preventive year-round and either an annual or semiannual blood test. The most common preventive is given once a month.

A flea bath is one means to rid a dog of fleas. Remember to treat not just the dog, but the environment (in and out of the home).

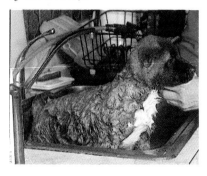

EXTERNAL PARASITES

Fleas

These pests are not only the dog's worst enemy but also enemy to the owner's pocketbook. Preventing is less expensive than treating, but regardless I think we'd prefer to spend our money elsewhere. I would guess that the majority of our dogs are allergic to the bite of a flea, and in many cases it only takes one flea bite. The protein in the flea's saliva is the culprit. Allergic dogs have a reaction, which usually results in a

Accustom the puppy to grooming at an early age. Akitas can be prone to "hot spots," which can be guarded against by good grooming habits as well as proper nutrition.

"hot spot." More than likely such a reaction will involve a trip to the veterinarian for treatment. Yes, good nutrition and prevention are less expensive. Fortunately today there are several good products available.

If there is a flea infestation, no one product is going to correct the problem. Not only will the dog require treatment so will the environment. In general flea collars are not very effective although there is now available an "egg" collar that will kill the eggs on the dog. Dips are the most economical but they are messy. There are some effective shampoos and treatments available through pet shops and veterinarians. An oral tablet arrived on the American market in 1995 and was popular in Europe the previous year. It sterilizes the female flea but will not kill adult fleas. Therefore the tablet, which is given monthly, will decrease the flea population but is not a "cure-all." Those dogs that suffer from flea-bite allergy will still be subjected to the bite of the flea. Another popular parasiticide is permethrin, which is applied to the back of the dog in one or two places depending on the dog's weight. This product works as a repellent causing the flea to get "hot feet" and jump off. Do not confuse this product with some of the organophosphates that are also applied to the dog's back.

Some products are not usable on young puppies. Treating fleas should be done under your veterinarian's guidance. Frequently it is necessary to combine products and the layman does not have the knowledge regarding possible toxicities. It is hard to believe but there are a few dogs that do have a natural resistance to fleas. Nevertheless it would be wise to treat all pets at the same time. Don't forget your cats. Cats just love to prowl the neighborhood and consequently return with unwanted guests.

Adult fleas live on the dog but their eggs drop off the dog into the environment. There they go through four larval stages before reaching adulthood, and thereby are able to jump back on the poor unsuspecting dog. The cycle resumes and takes between 21 to 28 days under ideal conditions. There are environmental products available that will kill both the adult fleas and the larvae.

Ticks

Ticks carry Rocky Mountain Spotted Fever, Lyme disease and can cause tick paralysis. They should be removed with tweezers, trying to pull out the head. The jaws carry disease. There is a tick preventive collar that does an excellent job. The ticks automatically back out on those dogs wearing collars.

Sarcoptic Mange

This is a mite that is difficult to find on skin scrapings. The pinnal reflex is a good indicator of this disease. Rub the ends of the pinna (ear) together and the dog will start scratching with his foot. Sarcoptes are highly contagious to other dogs and to humans although they do not live long on humans. They cause intense itching.

Demodectic Mange
This is a mite that is passed from the dam to her puppies. It affects youngsters age three to ten months. Diagnosis is confirmed by skin scraping. Small areas of alopecia around the eyes, lips and/or forelegs become visible. There is little itching unless there is a secondary bacterial infection. Some breeds are afflicted more than others.

Ear care for the Akita requires little more than removing debris from the external ear. Fortunately dogs with upright-standing ears are less prone to ear problems than drop-eared dogs.

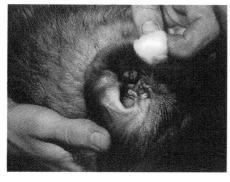

Cheyletiella
This causes intense itching and is diagnosed by skin scraping. It lives in the outer layers of the skin of dogs, cats, rabbits and humans. Yellow-gray scales may be found on the back and the rump, top of the head and the nose.

To Breed or Not To Breed
More than likely your breeder has requested that you have your puppy neutered or spayed. Your breeder's request is based on what is healthiest for your dog and what is most beneficial for your breed. Experienced and conscientious breeders devote many years into developing a bloodline. In order to do this, he makes every effort to plan each breeding in regard to conformation, temperament and health. This type of breeder does his best to perform the necessary testing (i.e., OFA, CERF, testing for inherited blood disorders, thyroid, etc.). Testing is expensive and sometimes very disheartening when a favorite dog doesn't pass his health tests. The health history pertains not only to the breeding stock but to the immediate ancestors. Reputable

breeders do not want their offspring to be bred indiscriminately. Therefore you may be asked to neuter or spay your puppy. Of course there is always the exception, and your breeder may agree to let you breed your dog under his direct supervision. This is an important concept. More and more effort is being made to breed healthier dogs.

Spay/Neuter

There are numerous benefits of performing this surgery at six months of age. Unspayed females are subject to mammary and ovarian cancer. In order to prevent mammary cancer she must be spayed prior to her first heat cycle. Later in life, an unspayed female may develop a pyometra (an infected uterus), which is definitely life threatening.

No bitch has ever been bred to top "Hatter," the grand dam of the Akita breed. Only top quality dogs should be bred for the sake of the breed's betterment.

Spaying is performed under a general anesthetic and is easy on the young dog. As you might expect it is a little harder on the older dog, but that is no reason to deny her the surgery. The surgery removes the ovaries and uterus. It is important to remove all the ovarian tissue. If some is left behind, she could remain attractive to males. In order to view the ovaries, a reasonably long incision is necessary. An ovariohysterectomy is considered major surgery.

World Famous judge from Japan, Dr. Nakazawa awards the Best of Breed at Taconic Hills Kennel Club.

Neutering the male at a young age will inhibit some characteristic male behavior that owners frown upon. I have found my boys will not hike their legs and mark territory if they are neutered at six months of age. Also neutering at a young age has hormonal benefits, lessening the chance of hormonal aggressiveness.

Surgery involves removing the testicles but leaving the scrotum. If there should be a retained testicle, then he definitely needs to be neutered before the age of two or three years. Retained testicles can develop into cancer. Unneutered males are at risk for testicular cancer, perineal fistulas, perianal tumors and fistulas and prostatic disease.

Intact males and females are prone to housebreaking accidents. Females urinate frequently before, during and after heat cycles, and males tend to mark territory if there is a female in heat. Males may show the same behavior if there is a visiting dog or guests.

Surgery involves a sterile operating procedure equivalent to human surgery. The incision site is shaved, surgically scrubbed and draped. The veterinarian wears a sterile surgical gown, cap, mask and gloves. Anesthesia should be monitored by a registered technician. It is customary for the veterinarian to recommend a pre-anesthetic blood screening, looking for metabolic problems and a ECG rhythm strip to check for normal heart function. Today anesthetics are equal to human anesthetics, which enables your dog to walk out of the clinic the same day as surgery.

Some folks worry about their dog gaining weight after being neutered or spayed. This is usually not the case. It is true that some dogs may be less active so they could develop a problem,

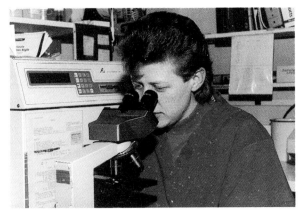

Veterinary science is advancing with amazing speed. Many veterinarians can offer same-day results from tests.

but my own dogs are just as active as they were before surgery. I have a hard time keeping weight on them. However, if your dog should begin to gain, then you need to decrease his food and see to it that he gets a little more exercise.

A spayed or neutered Akita may live a longer, healthier life than an unaltered dog. For large dogs, Akitas have promising life expectancies.

MEDICAL PROBLEMS

Anal Sacs

These are small sacs on either side of the rectum that can cause the dog discomfort when they are full. They should empty when the dog has a bowel movement. Symptoms of inflammation or impaction are excessive licking under the tail and/or a bloody or sticky discharge from the anal area. Breeders like myself recommend emptying the sacs on a regular schedule when bathing the dog. Many veterinarians prefer this isn't done unless there are symptoms. You can express the sacs by squeezing the two sacs (at the five and seven o'clock positions) in and up toward the anus. Take precautions not to get in the way of the foul-smelling fluid that is expressed. Some dogs object to this procedure so it would be wise to have someone hold the head. Scooting is caused by anal-sac irritation and not worms.

Colitis

The stool may be frank blood or blood tinged and is the result of inflammation of the colon. Colitis, sometimes intermittent, can be the result of stress, undiagnosed whipworms, or perhaps idiopathic (no explainable reason). I have had several dogs prone to this disorder. They felt fine and were willing to eat but would have intermittent bloody stools. If this is an ongoing problem, you should probably feed a diet higher in fiber. Seek professional help if your dog feels poorly and/or the condition persists.

Conjunctivitis

Many breeds are prone to this problem. The conjunctiva is the pink tissue that lines the inner surface of the eyeball except the clear, transparent cornea. Irritating substances such as bacteria, foreign matter or chemicals can cause it to become reddened and swollen. It is important to keep any hair trimmed from around the eyes. Long hair stays damp and aggravates the problem. Keep the eyes cleaned with warm water and wipe away any matter that has accumulated in the corner of the eyes. If the condition persists, you should see your veterinarian. This problem goes hand in hand with keratoconjunctivitis sicca.

Ear Infection

Otitis externa is an inflammation of the external ear canal that begins at the outside opening of the ear and extends inward to the eardrum. Dogs with pendulous ears are prone to this disease, but isn't it interesting that breeds with upright ears also have a high incidence of problems? Allergies, food and inhalant, along with hormonal

An Akita's eyes can be very sensitive. Keep the eyes clean and be sure to wipe away any accumulated matter. Owner, Ed Israel.

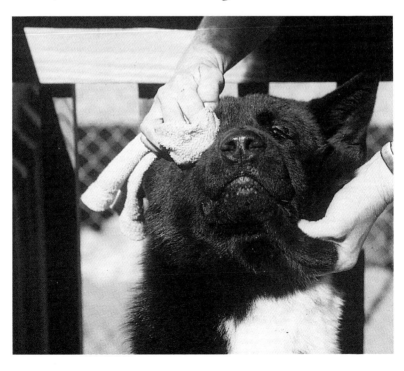

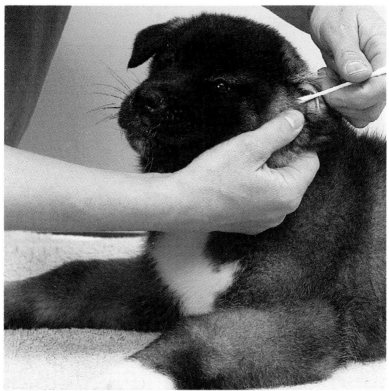

Don't probe in your puppy's ear any further than you can see. Ear mites are common with any breed. Should you detect dirt accumulation, your veterinarian can prescribe a treatment.

problems, such as hypothyroidism, are major contributors to the disease. For those dogs which have recurring problems you need to investigate the underlying cause if you hope to cure them.

I recommend that you are careful never to get water into the ears. Water provides a great medium for bacteria to grow. If your dog swims or you inadvertently get water into his ears, then use a drying agent. An at-home preparation would be to use equal parts of three-percent hydrogen peroxide and 70-percent rubbing alcohol. Another preparation is equal parts of white vinegar and water. Your veterinarian alternatively can provide a suitable product. When cleaning the ears, be careful of using cotton tip applicators since they make it easy to pack debris down into the canal. Only clean what you can see.

If your dog has an ongoing infection, don't be surprised if your veterinarian recommends sedating him and flushing his ears with a bulb syringe. Sometimes this needs to be done a few times to get the ear clean. The ear must be clean so that medication can come in contact with the canal. Be prepared to return for rechecks until the infection is gone. This may involve more flushings if the ears are very bad.

For chronic or recurring cases, your veterinarian may recommend thyroid testing, etc., and a hypoallergenic diet for a trial period of 10 to 12 weeks. Depending on your dog, it may be a good idea to see a dermatologist. Ears shouldn't be taken lightly. If the condition gets out of hand, then surgery may be necessary. Please ask your veterinarian to explain proper ear maintenance for your dog.

Flea Bite Allergy

This is the result of a hypersensitivity to the bite of a flea and its saliva. It only takes one bite to cause the dog to chew or scratch himself raw. Your dog may need medical attention to ease his discomfort. You need to clip the hair around the "hot spot" and wash it with a mild soap and water and you may need to do this daily if the area weeps. Apply an antibiotic anti-inflammatory product. Hot spots can occur from other trauma, such as grooming.

Fleas can be more than an annoying itch. Some Akitas can be hypersensitive to the bite of a flea, and any such allergic dog may need veterinary care to help relieve its discomfort.

Interdigital Cysts

Check for these on your dog's feet if he shows signs of lameness. They are frequently associated with staph infections and can be quite painful. A home remedy is to soak the infected foot in a solution of a half teaspoon of bleach in a couple of quarts of water. Do this two to three times a day for a couple of days. Check with your veterinarian for an alternative remedy; antibiotics usually work well as do zinc and vitiamin C supplements. If there is a recurring problem, surgery may be required.

Akitas generally do not like to have their feet touched. If accustomed to this from an early age, your adult Akita will be more tolerant and not become too unruffled.

Lameness

It may only be an interdigital cyst or it could be a mat between the toes, especially if your dog licks his feet. Sometimes it is hard to determine which

"Hey, that's my foot you're playing with!"

leg is affected. If he is holding up his leg, then you need to see your veterinarian.

Skin

Frequently poor skin is the result of an allergy to fleas, an inhalant allergy or food allergy. These types of problems usually result in a staph dermatitis. Dogs with food allergy usually show signs of severe itching and scratching. However, I have had some dogs with food allergies that never once itched. Their only symptom was swelling of the ears with no ear infection. Food allergy may result in recurrent bacterial skin and ear infections. Your veterinarian or dermatologist will recommend a good restricted diet. It is not wise for you to hit and miss with different dog foods. Many of the diets offered over the counter are not the hypoallergenic diet you are led to believe. Dogs acquire allergies through exposure.

Skin problems rarely plague Akitas from good breeding who have responsible owners who feed and groom properly. Breeding and feeding play key roles: first you breed a coat, then you feed a coat.

Inhalant allergies result in atopy, which causes licking of the feet, scratching the body and rubbing the muzzle. It may be seasonable. Your veterinarian or dermatologist can perform intradermal testing for inhalant allergies. If your dog should test positive, then a vaccine may be prepared. The results are very satisfying.

Tonsillitis

Usually young dogs have a higher incidence of this problem than the older ones. The older dogs have built up resistance. It is very contagious. Sometimes it is difficult to determine if it is tonsillitis or kennel cough since the symptoms are similar. Symptoms include fever, poor eating, swallowing with difficulty and retching up a white, frothy mucus.

DENTAL CARE for Your Dog's Life

So you've got a new puppy! You also have a new set of puppy teeth in your household. Anyone who has ever raised a puppy is abundantly aware of these new teeth. Your puppy will chew anything it can reach, chase your shoelaces, and play "tear the rag" with any piece of clothing it can find. When puppies are newly born, they have no teeth. At about four weeks of age, puppies of most breeds begin to develop their deciduous or baby teeth. They begin eating semi-solid food, fighting and biting with their litter mates, and learning discipline from their mother. As their new teeth come in, they inflict more pain on their mother's breasts, so her feeding sessions become less frequent and shorter. By six or eight weeks, the mother will start growling to warn her pups when they are fighting too roughly or hurting her as they nurse too much with their new teeth.

Puppies need to chew. It is a necessary part of their physical and mental development. They develop muscles and necessary life skills as they drag objects around, fight over possession, and vocalize alerts and warnings. Puppies chew on things to explore their world. They are using their sense of taste to determine what is food and what is not. How else can they tell an electrical cord from a lizard? At about four months of age, most puppies begin shedding their baby teeth. Often these teeth need some help to come out and make way for the permanent teeth. The incisors (front teeth) will be replaced

Akitas are naturally powerful chewers. Nylabones® are the strongest and safest pacifiers available. The O'BJ Akitas have benefited from Nylabones® for years and gladly recommend them for puppies and adults alike.

first. Then, the adult canine or fang teeth erupt. When the baby tooth is not shed before the permanent tooth comes in, veterinarians call it a retained deciduous tooth. This condition will often cause gum infections by trapping hair and debris between the permanent tooth and the retained baby tooth. Nylafloss® is an excellent device for puppies to use. They can toss it, drag it, and chew on the many surfaces it

The Hercules™ Bone from Nylabone® is strong enough for superhero Akitas.

Many dental devices are more than toys. Be sure your Akita's rope toy is made of nylon so that it is not destructible or corroding.

presents. The baby teeth can catch in the nylon material, aiding in their removal. Puppies that have adequate chew toys will have less destructive behavior, develop more physically, and have less chance of retained deciduous teeth.

During the first year, your dog

should be seen by your veterinarian at regular intervals. Your veterinarian will let you know when to bring in your puppy for vaccinations and parasite examinations. At each visit, your veterinarian should inspect the lips, teeth, and mouth as part of a complete physical examination. You should take some part in the maintenance of your dog's oral health. You should examine your dog's mouth weekly throughout his first year to make sure there are no sores, foreign objects, tooth problems, etc. If your dog drools excessively, shakes its head, or has bad breath, consult your veterinarian. By the time your dog is six months old, the permanent teeth are all in and plaque can start to accumulate on the tooth surfaces. This is when your dog needs to develop good dental-care habits to prevent calculus build-up on its teeth. Brushing is best. That is a fact that cannot be denied. However, some dogs do not like their teeth brushed regularly, or you may not be able to accomplish the task. In that case, you should consider a product that will help prevent plaque and calculus build-up.

The Plaque Attackers® and Galileo Bone® are other excellent choices for the first three years of a dog's life. Their shapes

Roar-Hide™ from Nylabone® is a unique molded rawhide treat—over 86% protein, it's digestible and delectable to dogs. Unlike regular rawhide which can be problematic, Roar-Hide™ is safe and effective in fighting tooth loss.

make them interesting for the dog. As the dog chews on them, the solid polyurethane massages the gums which improves the blood circulation to the

Akita puppies welcome the softer polyurethane Gumabone®. These devices prevent plaque and tartar build-up, develop the jaw bones, and amuse the ever-curious Akita urchin.

periodontal tissues. Projections on the chew devices increase the surface and are in contact with the tooth for more efficient cleaning. The unique shape and consistency prevent your dog from exerting excessive force on his own teeth or from breaking off pieces of the bone. If your dog is an aggressive chewer or weighs more than 55 pounds (25 kg), you should consider giving him a Nylabone®, the most durable chew product on the market.

Gumabones®, made by the Nylabone Company, areconstructed of strong polyurethane, which is softer than nylon. Less powerful chewers prefer the Gumabones® to the Nylabones®. A super option for your dog is the Hercules Bone®, a uniquely shaped bone named after the great Olympian for its exception strength. Like all Nylabone products, they are specially scented to make them attractive to your dog. Ask your veterinarian about these bones and he will validate the good doctor's prescription: Nylabones® not only give your dog a good chewing workout but also help to save your dog's teeth (and even his life, as it protects him from possible fatal periodontal diseases).

By the time dogs are four years old, 75% of them have periodontal disease. It is the most common infection in dogs.

The Nylaring® offers countless hours of diversion for your Akita puppy. It's safe and long-lasting and made of durable nylon.

Yearly examinations by your veterinarian are essential to maintaining your dog's good health. If your veterinarian detects periodontal disease, he or she may recommend a prophylactic cleaning. To do a thorough cleaning, it will be necessary to put your dog under anesthesia. With modern gas anesthetics and monitoring equipment, the procedure is pretty safe. Your veterinarian will scale the teeth with an ultrasound scaler or hand instrument. This removes the calculus from the teeth. If there are calculus deposits below the gum line, the veterinarian will plane the roots to make them smooth. After all of the calculus has been removed, the teeth are polished with pumice in a polishing cup. If any medical or surgical treatment is needed, it is done at this time. The final step would be fluoride treatment and your follow-up treatment at home. If the periodontal disease is advanced, the veterinarian may prescribe a medicated mouth rinse or antibiotics for use at home. Make sure your dog has safe, clean and attractive chew toys and treats. Chooz® treats are another way of using a consumable treat to help keep your dog's teeth clean.

Rawhide is the most popular of all materials for a dog to chew. This has never been good news to dog owners, because rawhide is inherently very dangerous for dogs. Thousands of dogs have died from rawhide, having swallowed the hide after it has become soft and mushy, only to cause stomach and

This Akita puppy will grow up with clean teeth, better breath, and positive play habits, thanks to Gumabone® and his thoughtful owner-breeder Ed Israel.

intestinal blockage. A new rawhide product on the market has finally solved the problem of rawhide: molded Roar-Hide™ from Nylabone. These are composed of processed, cut up, and melted American rawhide injected into your dog's favorite shape: a dog bone. These dog-safe devices smell and taste like rawhide but don't break up. The ridges on the bones help to fight tartar build-up on the teeth and they last ten times longer than the usual rawhide chews.

As your dog ages, professional examination and cleaning should become more frequent. The mouth should be inspected at least once a year. Your veterinarian may recommend visits every six months. In the geriatric patient, organs such as the heart, liver, and kidneys do not function as well as when they were young. Your veterinarian will

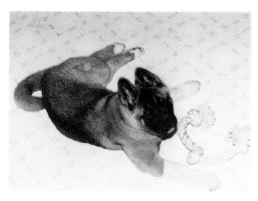

Be sure to offer your Akita puppy nylon rope toys. Cotton rope toys don't last nearly as long and since cotton is organic, it rots and collects microscopic debris. Look for the Nylafloss®—it's the best option for rope devices.

probably want to test these organs' functions prior to using general anesthesia for dental cleaning. If your dog is a good chewer and you work closely with your veterinarian, your dog can keep all of its teeth all of its life. However, as your dog ages, his sense of smell, sight, and taste will diminish. He may not have the desire to chase, trap or chew his toys. He will also not have the energy to chew for long periods, as arthritis and periodontal disease make chewing painful. This will leave you with more responsibility for keeping his teeth clean and healthy. The dog that would not let you brush his teeth at one year of age, may let you brush his teeth now that he is ten years old.

A mouthful of Hercules! The raised dental tips on the Hercules Bone™ provide added chewing stimulation. The bone is uniquely shaped so that there is no cross-section, making the entire device chewable and helpful.

If you train your dog with good chewing habits as a puppy, he will have healthier teeth throughout his life.

IDENTIFICATION and Finding the Lost Dog

There are several ways of identifying your dog. The old standby is a collar with dog license, rabies, and ID tags. Unfortunately collars have a way of being separated from the dog and tags fall off. I am not suggesting you shouldn't use a collar and tags. If they stay intact and on the dog, they are the quickest way of identification.

For several years owners have been tattooing their dogs. Some tattoos use a number with a registry. Here lies the problem because there are several registries to check. If you wish to tattoo, use your social security number. The humane shelters have the means to trace it. It is usually done on the inside of the rear thigh. The area is first shaved and numbed. There is no pain, although a few dogs do not like the buzzing sound. Occasionally tattooing is not legible and needs to be redone.

The newest method of identification is microchipping. The microchip is a computer chip that is no larger than a grain of rice. The veterinarian implants it by injection between the shoulder blades. The dog feels no discomfort. If your dog is lost and picked up by the humane society, they can trace you by scanning the microchip, which has its own code. Microchip scanners are friendly to other brands of microchips and their registries. The microchip comes with a dog tag saying the dog is microchipped. It is the safest way of identifying your dog.

FINDING THE LOST DOG

I am sure you will agree with me that there would be little worse than losing your dog. Responsible pet owners rarely lose their dogs. They do not let their dogs run free because they don't want harm to come to them. Not only that but in most, if not all, states there is a leash law.

Beware of fenced-in yards. They can be a hazard. Dogs find ways to escape either over or under the fence. Another fast exit is through the gate that perhaps the neighbor's child left unlocked.

Below is a list that hopefully will be of help to you if you need it. Remember don't give up, keep looking. Your dog is worth your efforts.

1. Contact your neighbors and put flyers with a photo on it in their mailboxes. Information you should include would be the dog's name, breed, sex, color, age, source of identification, when your dog was last seen and where, and your name and phone numbers. It may be helpful to say the dog needs medical care. Offer a *reward*.

2. Check all local shelters daily. It is also possible for your dog to be picked up away from home and end up in an out-of-the-way shelter. Check these too. Go in person. It is not good enough to call. Most shelters are limited on the time they can hold dogs then they are put up for adoption or euthanized. There is the possibility that your dog will not make it to the shelter for several days. Your dog could have been wandering or someone may have tried to keep him.

3. Notify all local veterinarians. Call and send flyers.

4. Call your breeder. Frequently breeders are contacted when one of their breed is found.

5. Contact the rescue group for your breed.

6. Contact local schools—children may have seen your dog.

7. Post flyers at the schools, groceries, gas stations, convenience stores, veterinary clinics, groomers and any other place that will allow them.

8. Advertise in the newspaper.

9. Advertise on the radio.

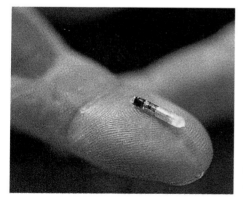

The newest method of identification is microchipping. The microchip is a computer chip that is no bigger than a grain of rice.

TRAVELING with Your Dog

The earlier you start traveling with your new puppy or dog, the better. He needs to become accustomed to traveling. However, some dogs are nervous riders and become carsick easily. It is helpful if he starts with an empty stomach. Do not despair, as it will go better if you continue taking him with you on short fun rides. How would you feel if every time you rode in the car you stopped at the doctor's for an injection? You would soon dread that nasty car. Older dogs that tend to get carsick may have more of a problem adjusting to traveling. Those dogs that are having a serious problem may benefit from some medication prescribed by the veterinarian.

Do give your dog a chance to relieve himself before getting into the car. It is a good idea to be prepared for a clean up with a leash, paper towels, bag and terry cloth towel.

The safest place for your dog is in a fiberglass crate, although close confinement can promote carsickness in some dogs. If your dog is nervous you can try letting him ride on the seat next to you or in someone's lap.

An alternative to the crate would be to use a car harness made for dogs and/or a safety strap attached to the harness or collar. Whatever you do, do not let your dog ride in the back of a pickup truck unless he is securely tied on a very short lead. I've seen trucks stop quickly and, even though the dog was tied, it fell out and was dragged.

Your puppy's safety depends entirely on you and the choices you make. Whether it's the kind of toys you provide or the way in which he travels, your Akita counts on your discretion.

Crates are a safe way to travel with your Akita. Akitas prefer wire crates to fiberglass ones because they like to see what's going on around them. Be sure the crate is large enough for the Akita. He will not tolerate being cramped and will find a way out in no time!

I do occasionally let my dogs ride loose with me because I really enjoy their companionship, but in all honesty they are safer in their crates. I have a friend whose van rolled in an accident but his dogs, in their fiberglass crates, were not injured nor did they escape. Another advantage of the crate is that it is a safe place to leave him if you need to run into the store. Otherwise you wouldn't be able to leave the windows down. Keep in mind that while many dogs are overly protective in their crates, this may not be enough to deter dognappers. In some states it is against the law to leave a dog in the car unattended.

Never leave a dog loose in the car wearing a collar and leash. I have known more than one dog that has killed himself by hanging. Do not let him put his head out an open window. Foreign debris can be blown into his eyes. When leaving your dog unattended in a car, consider the temperature. It can take less than five minutes to reach temperatures over 100 degrees Fahrenheit.

TRIPS

Perhaps you are taking a trip. Give consideration to what is best for your dog–traveling with you or boarding. When traveling by car, van or motor home, you need to think ahead about locking your vehicle. In all probability you have many valuables in the car and do not wish to leave it unlocked. Perhaps most valuable and not replaceable is your dog. Give thought to securing your vehicle and providing adequate ventilation for him. Another consideration for you when traveling with your dog is medical problems that may arise and little inconveniences, such as exposure to external parasites. Some areas of the country are quite flea infested. You may want to carry flea spray with you. This is even a good idea when staying in motels. Quite possibly you are not the only occupant of the room.

There's a parade in town and there's an Akita leading the way. This is Pat Happel with Chocin's Merriac showing off what fun Akitas can have in the community.

Unbelievably many motels and even hotels do allow canine guests, even some very first-class ones. Gaines Pet Foods Corporation publishes *Touring With Towser*, a directory of domestic hotels and motels that accommodate guests with dogs. Their address is Gaines TWT, PO Box 5700, Kankakee, IL, 60902. I would recommend you call ahead to any motel that you may be considering and see if they accept pets. Sometimes it is necessary to pay a deposit against room damage. Of course you are more likely to gain accommodations for a small dog than a large dog. Also the management feels reassured when you mention that your dog will be crated. Since my dogs tend to bark when I leave the room, I leave the TV on nearly full blast to deaden the noises outside that tend to encourage my dogs to bark. If you do travel with your dog, take along plenty of baggies so that you can clean up after him. When we all do our share in cleaning up, we make it possible for motels to continue accepting our pets. As a matter of fact, you should practice cleaning up everywhere you take your dog.

Depending on where your are traveling, you may need an up-to-date health certificate issued by your veterinarian.

It is good policy to take along your dog's medical information, which would include the name, address and phone number of your veterinarian, vaccination record, rabies certificate, and any medication he is taking.

AIR TRAVEL

When traveling by air, you need to contact the airlines to check their policy. Usually you have to make arrangements up to a couple of weeks in advance for traveling with your dog. The airlines require your dog to travel in an airline approved fiberglass crate. Usually these can be purchased through the airlines but they are also readily available in most pet-supply stores. If your dog is not accustomed to a crate, then it is a good idea to get him acclimated to it before your trip. The day of the actual trip you should withhold water about one hour ahead of departure and no food for about 12 hours. The airlines

If you are intending to show the puppy, acclimating it to a crate is necessary. This prepares him for trips to and from shows as well as speeds up the housebreaking process.

generally have temperature restrictions, which do not allow pets to travel if it is either too cold or too hot. Frequently these restrictions are based on the temperatures at the departure and arrival airports. It's best to inquire about a health certificate. These usually need to be issued within ten days of departure. You should arrange for non-stop, direct flights and if a commuter plane should be involved, check to see if it will carry dogs. Some don't. The Humane Society of the United States has put together a tip sheet for airline traveling. You can receive a copy by sending a self-addressed stamped envelope to:

The Humane Society of the United States
Tip Sheet
2100 L Street NW
Washington, DC 20037.

Adult Akitas will perfectly accept the confines of their crate if accustomed to the crate from puppyhood. Akitas think of their crates as their dens: they will not accept visitors inside their crates so it's best for friends to stay nearby.

Regulations differ for traveling outside of the country and are sometimes changed without notice. Well in advance you need to write or call the appropriate consulate or agricultural department for instructions. Some countries have lengthy quarantines (six months), and countries differ in their rabies vaccination requirements. For instance, it may have to be given at least 30 days ahead of your departure.

Do make sure your dog is wearing proper identification. You never know when you might be in an accident and

separated from your dog. Or your dog could be frightened and somehow manage to escape and run away. When I travel, my dogs wear collars with engraved nameplates with my name, phone number and city. Another suggestion would be to carry in-case-of-emergency instructions. These would include the address and phone number of a relative or friend, your veterinarian's name, address and phone number, and your dog's medical information.

BOARDING KENNELS

Perhaps you have decided that you need to board your dog. Your veterinarian can recommend a good boarding facility or possibly a pet sitter that will come to your house. It is customary for the boarding kennel to ask for proof of vaccination for the DHLPP, rabies and bordetella vaccine. The bordetella should have been given within six months of boarding. This is for your protection. If they do not ask for this proof I would not board at their kennel. Ask about flea control. Those dogs that suffer flea-bite allergy can get in trouble at a boarding kennel. Unfortunately boarding kennels are limited on how much they are able to do.

For more information on pet sitting, contact NAPPS: National Association of Professional Pet Sitters
1200 G Street, NW
Suite 760
Washington, DC 20005.

Our clinic has technicians that pet sit and technicians that board clinic patients in their homes. This may be an alternative for you. Ask your veterinarian if they have an employee that can help you. There is a definite advantage of having a technician care for your dog, especially if your dog is on medication or is a senior citizen.

You can write for a copy of *Traveling With Your Pet* from ASPCA, Education Department, 441 E. 92nd Street, New York, NY 10128.

Ch. Ko-Son is practically naked for this win handled by the well-dressed James Taylor. Proficient handling and proper grooming can give even an out-of-coat Akita the winning edge.

BEHAVIOR and Canine Communication

Studies of the human/animal bond point out the importance of the unique relationships that exist between people and their pets. Those of us who share our lives with pets understand the special part they play through companionship, service and protection.

Senior citizens show more concern for their own eating habits when they have the responsibility of feeding a dog. Seeing that their dog is routinely exercised encourages the owner to think of schedules that otherwise may seem unimportant to the senior citizen. The older owner may be arthritic and feeling poorly but with responsibility for his dog he has a reason to get up and get moving. It is a big plus if his dog is an attention seeker who will demand such from his owner.

Over the last couple of decades, it has been shown that pets relieve the stress of those who lead busy lives. Owning a pet has been known to lessen the occurrence of heart attack and stroke.

Many single folks thrive on the companionship of a dog. Lifestyles are very different from a long time ago, and today more individuals seek the single life. However, they receive fulfillment from owning a dog.

Most likely the majority of our dogs live in family environments. The companionship they provide is well worth the effort involved. In my opinion, every child should have the opportunity to have a family dog. Dogs teach responsibility through understanding their care, feelings and even respecting their life cycles. Frequently those children who have not been exposed to dogs grow up afraid of dogs, which isn't good. Dogs sense timidity and some will take advantage of the situation.

Today more dogs are serving as service dogs. Since the origination of the Seeing Eye dogs years ago, we now have trained hearing dogs. Also dogs are trained to provide service for the handicapped and are able to perform many different tasks for their owners. Search and Rescue dogs, with their handlers, are sent throughout the world to assist in recovery of disaster victims. They are life savers.

Therapy dogs are very popular with nursing homes, and some hospitals even allow them to visit. The inhabitants truly look forward to their visits. Judy Iby says, "I have taken a couple of my dogs visiting and left in tears when I saw the response of the patients. They wanted and were allowed to have my dogs in their beds to hold and love."

Nationally there is a Pet Awareness Week to educate students and others about the value and basic care of our pets. Many countries take an even greater interest in their pets than Americans do. In those countries the pets are allowed to accompany their owners into restaurants and shops, etc. In the U.S. this freedom is only available to our service dogs. Even so we think very highly of the human/animal bond.

Akitas participate in therapy work within their communities as lovingly demonstrated by Maria Heldman's dog in a local convalescent center.

CANINE BEHAVIOR

Canine behavior problems are the number-one reason for pet owners to dispose of their dogs, either through

new homes, humane shelters or euthanasia. Unfortunately there are too many owners who are unwilling to devote the necessary time to properly train their dogs. On the other hand, there are those who not only are concerned about inherited health problems but are also aware of the dog's mental stability.

You may realize that a breed and his group relatives (i.e., sporting, hounds, etc.) show tendencies to behavioral characteristics. An experienced breeder can acquaint you with his breed's personality. Unfortunately many breeds are labeled with poor temperaments when actually the breed as a whole is not affected but only a small percentage of individuals within the breed.

If the breed in question is very popular, then of course there may be a higher number of unstable dogs. Do not label a breed good or bad. I know of absolutely awful-tempered dogs within one of our most popular, lovable breeds.

Inheritance and environment contribute to the dog's behavior. Some naïve people suggest inbreeding as the cause of bad temperaments. Inbreeding only results in poor behavior if the

Good temperaments are passed from parent to offspring. Akita breeders carefully consider which dogs are sound enough— physically and temperamentally—to use in breeding programs.

ancestors carry the trait. If there are excellent temperaments behind the dogs, then inbreeding will promote good temperaments in the offspring. Did you ever consider that inbreeding is what sets the characteristics of a breed? A purebred dog is the end result of inbreeding. This does not spare the mixed-breed dog from the same problems. Mixed-breed dogs frequently are the offspring of purebred dogs.

When planning a breeding, I like to observe the potential stud and his offspring in the show ring. If I see unruly behavior, I try to look into it further. I want to know if it is genetic or environmental, due to the lack of training and socialization. A good breeder will avoid breeding mentally unsound dogs.

Littermates share more than two parents, as these Yakedo Akitas demonstrate. They share temperaments, appearances, genetic makeup, and that Akita air of distinction.

Not too many decades ago most of our dogs led a different lifestyle than what is prevalent today. Usually mom stayed home so the dog had human companionship and someone to discipline it if needed. Not much was expected from the dog. Today's mom works and everyone's life is at a much faster pace.

The dog may have to adjust to being a "weekend" dog. The family is gone all day during the week, and the dog is left to his own devices for entertainment. Some dogs sleep all day waiting for their family to come home and others become wigwam wreckers if given the opportunity. Crates do ensure the safety of the dog and the house. However, he could become physically and emotionally crippled if he doesn't get enough exercise and attention. We still appreciate and want the companionship of our dogs although we expect more from them. In many cases we tend to forget dogs are just that—*dogs* not human beings.

Dogs accept their crates as their personal "houses" and seem to be content with their routine and thrive on trying their best to please me.

SOCIALIZING AND TRAINING

Many prospective puppy buyers lack experience regarding the proper socialization and training needed to develop the type of pet we all desire. In the first 18 months, training does take some work. Trust me, it is easier to start proper training before there is a problem that needs to be corrected.

The initial work begins with the breeder. The breeder should start socializing the puppy at five to six weeks of age and cannot let up. Human socializing is critical up through 12 weeks of age and likewise important during the following months. The litter should be left together during the first few weeks but it is necessary to separate them by ten weeks of age. Leaving them together after that time will increase competition for litter dominance. If puppies are not socialized with people by 12 weeks of age, they will be timid in later life.

The eight- to ten-week age period is a fearful time for puppies. They need to be handled very gently around children and adults. There should be no harsh discipline during this time. Starting at 14 weeks of

Akita puppies learn the rules of the pack, that is, how to get along with other canines. Litter socialization exposes puppies to laws of the "alpha" dog, the leader of the pack.

Akita puppies need the opportunity to meet humans. When properly socialized with people—big and small—Akitas willingly accept them as members of the pack, one of the family. These fur babies are three-and-a-half weeks of age.

age, the puppy begins the juvenile period, which ends when he reaches sexual maturity around six to 14 months of age. During the juvenile period he needs to be introduced to strangers (adults, children and other dogs) on the home property. At sexual maturity he will begin to bark at strangers and become more protective. Males start to lift their legs to urinate but if you desire you can inhibit this behavior by walking your boy on leash away from trees, shrubs, fences, etc.

Perhaps you are thinking about an older puppy. You need to inquire about the puppy's social experience. If he has lived in a kennel, he may have a hard time adjusting to people and environmental stimuli. Assuming he has had a good social upbringing, there are advantages to an older puppy.

Training includes puppy kindergarten and a minimum of one to two basic training classes. During these classes you will learn how to dominate your youngster. This is especially important if you own a large breed of dog. It is somewhat harder, if not nearly impossible, for some owners to be the Alpha figure when their dog towers over them. You will be taught how to properly restrain your dog. This concept is important. Again it puts you in the Alpha position. All dogs need to be restrained many times during their lives. Believe it or not, some of our worst offenders are the eight-week-old puppies that are brought to our clinic. They need to be gently restrained for a nail trim but the way they carry on you would think we were killing them. In comparison, their vaccination is a "piece of cake." When we ask dogs to do something that is not agreeable to them, then their worst comes out. Life will be easier for your dog if you expose him at a young age to the necessities of life—proper behavior and restraint.

UNDERSTANDING THE DOG'S LANGUAGE

Most authorities agree that the dog is a descendent of the wolf. The dog and wolf have similar traits. For instance both are pack oriented and prefer not to be isolated for long periods of time. Another characteristic is that the dog, like the wolf, looks to the leader—Alpha—for direction. Both the wolf and the dog communicate through body language, not only within their pack but with outsiders.

Every pack has an Alpha figure. The dog looks to you, or should look to you, to be that leader. If your dog doesn't receive the proper training and guidance, he very well may replace you as Alpha. This would be a serious problem and is certainly a disservice to your dog.

Eye contact is one way the Alpha wolf keeps order within his pack. You are Alpha so you must establish eye contact with your puppy. Obviously your puppy will have to look at you. Practice eye contact even if you need to hold his head for five to ten seconds at a time. You can give him a treat as a reward. Make sure your eye contact is gentle and not threatening. Later, if he has been naughty, it is permissible to give him a long, penetrating look. I caution you there are some older dogs that never learned eye contact as puppies and cannot accept eye contact. You should avoid eye contact with these dogs since they feel threatened and will retaliate as such.

BODY LANGUAGE

The play bow, when the forequarters are down and the hindquarters are elevated, is an invitation to play. Puppies play fight, which helps them learn the acceptable limits of biting. This is necessary for later in their lives. Nevertheless, an owner may be falsely reassured by the playful nature of his dog's aggression. Playful aggression toward another dog or human may be an indication of serious aggression in the future. Owners should never play fight or play tug-of-war with any dog that is inclined to be dominant.

An Akita on his back, with his belly exposed, submits to his owner's dominant role....a good tummy rub is one of the benefits of being subordinate to an alpha master.

Signs of submission are:

    1.   Avoids eye contact.

    2.   Active submission—the dog crouches down, ears back and the tail is lowered.

    3. Passive submission—the dog rolls on his side with his hindlegs in the air and frequently urinates.

Signs of dominance are:

    1. Makes eye contact.

    2. Stands with ears up, tail up and the hair raised on his neck.

    3. Shows dominance over another dog by standing at right angles over it.

Dominant dogs tend to behave in characteristic ways such as:

    1. The dog may be unwilling to move from his place (i.e., reluctant to give up the sofa if the owner wants to sit there).

2. He may not part with toys or objects in his mouth and may show possessiveness with his food bowl.

3. He may not respond quickly to commands.

4. He may be disagreeable for grooming and dislikes to be petted.

Dogs are popular because of their sociable nature. Those that have contact with humans during the first 12 weeks of life regard them as a member of their own species—their pack. All dogs have the potential for both dominant and submissive behavior. Only through experience and training do they learn to whom it is appropriate to show which behavior. Not all dogs are concerned with dominance but owners need to be aware of that potential. It is wise for the owner to establish his dominance early on.

A human can express dominance or submission toward a dog in the following ways:

1. Meeting the dog's gaze signals dominance. Averting the gaze signals submission. If the dog growls or threatens, averting the gaze is the first avoiding action to take—it may prevent attack. It is important to establish eye contact in the puppy. The older dog that has not been exposed to eye contact may see it as a threat and will not be willing to submit.

2. Being taller than the dog signals dominance; being lower signals submission. This is why, when attempting to make friends with a strange dog or catch the runaway, one should kneel down to his level. Some owners see their dogs become dominant when allowed on the furniture or

Akitas take eye contact very seriously. An Akita that acknowledges your alpha role will not meet your eyes. When an Akita stares directly at you, he is challenging your position as alpha.

on the bed. Then he is at the owner's level.

3. An owner can gain dominance by ignoring all the dog's social initiatives. The owner pays attention to the dog only when he obeys a command.

No dog should be allowed to achieve dominant status over any adult or child. Ways of preventing are as follows:

1. Handle the puppy gently, especially during the three- to four-month period.

Pay attention to your Akita only when he obeys your command. Praise him and teach him that pleasing you makes his world ever more pleasant. Remember that a disobedient Akita is never right.

2. Let the children and adults handfeed him and teach him to take food without lunging or grabbing.

3. Do not allow him to chase children or joggers.

4. Do not allow him to jump on people or mount their legs. Even females may be inclined to mount. It is not only a male habit.

5. Do not allow him to growl for any reason.

6. Don't participate in wrestling or tug-of-war games.

7. Don't physically punish puppies for aggressive behavior. Restrain him from repeating the infraction and teach an alternative behavior. Dogs should earn everything they receive from their owners. This would include sitting to receive petting or treats, sitting before going out the door and sitting to receive the collar and leash. These types of exercises reinforce the owner's dominance.

Young children should never be left alone with a dog. It is important that children learn some basic obedience commands so they have some control over the dog. They will gain the respect of their dog.

FEAR

One of the most common problems dogs experience is being fearful. Some dogs are more afraid than others. On the lesser side, which is sometimes humorous to watch, my dog can be afraid of a strange object. He acts silly when something is out of place in the house. I call his problem perceptive intelligence. He realizes the abnormal within his known environment. He does not react the same way in strange environments since he does not know what is normal.

On the more serious side is a fear of people. This can result in backing off, seeking his own space and saying "leave me alone" or it can result in an aggressive behavior that may lead to challenging the person. Respect that the dog wants to be left alone and give him time to come forward. If you approach the cornered dog, he may resort to

When training an Akita, it is inadvisable to lie down with the puppy. By lowering yourself to the dog's level, he may perceive you as his equal. Always remain higher than the Akita student. Owner, Edward J. Finnegan.

snapping. If you leave him alone, he may decide to come forward, which should be rewarded with a treat. Years ago we had a dog that behaved in this manner. We coaxed people to stop by the house and make friends with our fearful dog. She learned to take the treats and after weeks of work she overcame her suspicions and made friends more readily.

Some dogs may initially be too fearful to take treats. In these cases it is helpful to make sure the dog hasn't eaten for about 24 hours. Being a little hungry encourages him to accept the treats, especially if they are of the "gourmet"

Some breeders subscribe to formal temperament testing in which the Akita is exposed to unknown elements (such as an opening umbrella) to observe how the dog reacts in each situation.

variety. I knew a dog that worries about strangers since people seldom stop by my house. Over the years she learned a cue and jumps up quickly to visit anyone sitting on the sofa. She learned by herself that all guests on the sofa were to be trusted friends. I think she felt more comfortable with them being at her level, rather than towering over her.

Dogs can be afraid of numerous things, including loud noises and thunderstorms. Invariably the owner rewards (by comforting) the dog when it shows signs of fearfulness. A friend had a terrible problem with a favorite dog in the Utility obedience class. Not only was he intimidated in the class but he was afraid of noise and afraid of displeasing. Frequently he would knock down the bar jump, which clattered dreadfully. She gave him credit because he continued to try to clear it, although he was terribly scared. She finally learned to "reward" him every time he knocked down the jump. She would jump up and down, clap my hands and tell him how great he was. Her psychology worked, he relaxed and eventually cleared the jump with ease. When your dog is frightened, direct his attention to something else and act happy. Don't dwell on his fright.

AGGRESSION

Some different types of aggression are: predatory, defensive, dominance, possessive, protective, fear induced, noise provoked, "rage" syndrome (unprovoked aggression), maternal and aggression directed toward other dogs. Aggression is the most common behavioral problem encountered. Protective breeds are expected to be more aggressive than others but with the proper upbringing they can make very dependable companions. You need to be able to read your dog.

Many factors contribute to aggression including genetics and environment. An improper environment, which may include the living conditions, lack of social life, excessive punishment, being attacked or frightened by an aggressive dog, etc., can all influence a dog's behavior. Even spoiling him and giving too much praise may be detrimental. Isolation and the lack of human contact or exposure to frequent teasing by children or adults also can ruin a good dog.

Lack of direction, fear, or confusion lead to aggression in those dogs that are so inclined. Any obedience exercise, even the sit and down, can direct the dog and overcome fear and/or confusion. Every dog should learn these commands as a youngster, and there should be periodic reinforcement.

When a dog is showing signs of aggression, you should speak calmly (no screaming or hysterics) and firmly give a command that he understands, such as the sit. As soon as your dog obeys, you have assumed your dominant position. Aggression presents a problem because there may be danger to others. Sometimes it is an emotional issue. Owners may consciously or unconsciously encourage their dog's aggression. Other owners show responsibility by accepting the problem and taking measures to keep it under control. The owner is responsible for his dog's actions, and it is not wise to take a chance on someone being bitten, especially a child. Euthanasia is the solution for some owners and in severe cases this may be the best choice. However, few dogs are that dangerous and very few are that much of a threat to their owners. If caution is exercised and professional help is gained early on, then I surmise most cases can be controlled.

Puppies learn the limits of aggression and biting in play with each other. Given the strength of the Akita, socialization and discipline make the difference between an unmanageable bear-slaying beast and a delightful, biddable companion animal.

Some authorities recommend feeding a lower protein (less than 20 percent) diet. They believe this can aid in reducing aggression. If the dog loses weight, then vegetable oil can be added. Veterinarians and

Provide Akita puppies with suitable playthings. The Nylafloss® is durable and safe and gives puppies an excellent means to work off stress— plus it's good for their incoming teeth.

behaviorists are having some success with pharmacology. In many cases treatment is possible and can improve the situation.

If you have done everything according to "the book" regarding training and socializing and are still having a behavior problem, don't procrastinate. It is important that the problem gets attention before it is out of hand. It is estimated that 20 percent of a veterinarian's time may be devoted to dealing with problems before they become so intolerable that the dog is separated from its home and owner. If your veterinarian isn't able to help, he should refer you to a behaviorist.

Visiting with Ch. The Joker Is Wild O'BJ, bred by the author, this is television star Betty White, well known for her involvement with animal groups and the dog fancy, and professional handler Papoose. Photograph taken in benching area at the Westminster Kennel Club. Courtesy of Roger Kaplan.

SUGGESTED READING

TS-175
The Most Complete
Dog Book Ever
Published
896 pages, over
1300 full-color
photos.

TS-257
Choosing A Dog
for Life
384 pages, over
700 full-color
photos.

KW-226
Shibas
192 pages, over
175 full-color
photos.

TS-249
Skin & Coat Care
for your Dog
224 pages, over 190
full-color photos.

TS-214
Owner's Guide to
Dog Health
432 pages, over 300
full-color photos.

TS-252
Dog Behavior and
Training
288 pages, nearly
200 full-color photos.

The World of the Akita

TS-256

The World of the Akita *by Barbara J. Andrews is the most comprehensive and colorful book on the breed ever published. Barbara J. Andrews, known as "BJ" to the Akita fancy, is the most successful breeder of Akitas in the world, having bred approximately 200 champions internationally. Over 400 pages in length,* The World of the Akita *contains hundreds of color photographs of the the great champions, dams and sires as well as detailed chapters on the origin of the Akita in Japan and the United States, the breed standard, Akita temperament and trainability, breeding, whelping and caring for puppies, showing, obedience, and general maintenance. The author, who is the originator of the Register of Merit system accepted by the Akita Club of America, introduces in this book the Akita Hall of Fame including the names and photographs the country's top dogs and breeders. Indispensable and definitive, this volume is absolutely breathtaking, as well as fascinating and challenging—just like the Akita dog himself!*

INDEX